WASHINGTON INTERNATIONAL UNIVERSITY

FORTY YEARS OF TANZANIA ECONOMIC PERFORMANCE: AN ANALYSIS OF ECONOMIC GROWTH AND DEVELOPMENT PATTERNS AND CONDITIONS FOR SUSTAINABLE POVERTY FREE ECONOMIC GROWTH

Thesis Presented in Fulfillment of
Requirements for Doctorate Degree Program of the
Washington International University

By

MARY MICHAEL NAGU

July, 2002

Berichte aus der Volkswirtschaft

Mary Michael Nagu

**Forty Years of Tanzania Economic Performance:
An Analysis of Economic Growth and Development
Patterns and Conditions for Sustainable Poverty Free
Economic Growth**

Shaker Verlag
Aachen 2006

Bibliographic information published by Die Deutsche Bibliothek
Die Deutsche Bibliothek lists this publication in the Deutsche
Nationalbibliografie; detailed bibliographic data is available in the internet at
http://dnb.ddb.de.

Zugl.: Washington International University, Diss., 2002

Printed in Germany.

ISBN-10: 3-8322-5067-0
ISBN-13: 978-3-8322-5067-6
ISSN 0945-1048

Shaker Verlag GmbH • P.O. BOX 101818 • D-52018 Aachen
Phone: 0049/2407/9596-0 • Telefax: 0049/2407/9596-9
Internet: www.shaker.de • eMail: info@shaker.de

ABSTRACT

Tanzania is one of the poorest countries in the world but it has great potential to develop given its rich resource endowment, political will, good economic policies and commitment. The country has also been receiving enormous assistance in the form of grants and loans from both multilateral and bilateral donors to improve its economic well-being. Yet forty years of economic struggle have not brought satisfactory progress as economic performance has remained dismal.

This study endeavors to establish the primary determinants of economic growth for Tanzania basing on the country's 40 years performance. The study employed the statistical analysis of secondary data covering the period from 1961 to 2000. The variables included in the study are, Gross Domestic Product (GDP), Total public investment in physical capital, Total public investment in human capital (government expenditures in health and education sectors), Trade (Exports & Imports), Population growth, Inflation, Tax distortion (ratio of revenue collection to GDP) and Total government expenditures. The statistical regression analysis used is the simple Ordinary Least Squares (OLS) method owing to its superiority over other methods.

With the aid of E-Views econometric software package, all variables except Tax distortion and Import trade were found to be positively related to economic growth. However the significance and coefficient values differ from one variable to another. In principle, however, the variables were found to have significant relationship with economic growth. At a conversional level therefore, these variables deduced from theoretical foundations highly account for Tanzania's economic growth.

Following the study's findings, policy recommendations are made in the conclusion of this study and of importance is that investment in human and physical capital should be fostered meanwhile tax distortion should be curbed. Moreover an analysis of imported goods should be carried out so as to avoid unnecessary leakages, which in a way stifle economic growth.

DEDICATION

I dedicate this Thesis to the poor particularly the toiling women, children and youth who form the poorest of the poor of Tanzanians.

ACKNOWLEDGEMENT

This work has benefited from the contributions of many individuals. To all of them I wish to express my heartfelt gratitude. I may not possibly exhaust the list in thanking them all. The few I will name will represent the endless list. First in the list is my thesis supervisor who not only read through the whole text and made a lot of constructive comments but also gave me a lot of encouragement to carry on with the task of completing the thesis. Dr. Michael Busler helped me immensely from the initial stage of proposal preparation to the final text of the thesis.

I want to thank two special personalities who were suggested to me by Prof. Felician Msambichaka through Dr. Henry Mambo, a colleague at the Civil Service Department. These are none other than Mr. Joseph Njau and Mr. Wilhelm Ngasamiaku who collected all the required data from various sources and compiled for me most of the required information. They also, with the use of software, worked out the Regression for me. The support given to my satisfaction by these two graduate students deserves my recognition and acknowledgement. Without the cooperation of Professor Felician Msambichaka and Dr. Henry Mambo it would have taken a lot of my effort to locate the two resourceful students. To Professor Felician Msambichaka and Dr. Henry Mambo I say I owe them my gratitude.

I am indebted to Professor Joseph Kuzilwa and Mr. Harrold Utouh of Mzumbe University (MU), Professor Talala Mbise, my colleague Member of Parliament, from Arumeru East in Arusha for their useful comments and for allocating their valuable time for that purpose. I also received a lot of encouragement from the Prime Minister Honourable Frederick Sumaye and my colleague Ministers, which increased my commitment to undertake the study.

The pride I always felt of my President's eloquent speeches on poverty eradication, which shows his commitment towards the fight against it, inspired me to go back to the books and found it to be a cardinal obligation from my part to join him in making a small

iii

contribution towards poverty eradication. I did enjoy the full support from Civil Service Department especially from the Permanent Secretary and the rest of the staff in particular my Personal Assistant, the two Secretaries, the Driver and the Attendant. To them I say thank you! My father and mother continued with their tireless support and encouragement; may God give them more years of life.

Finally and not the least is my heartfelt gratitude to my husband Professor Joseph Nagu who without hesitation, but with a lot of affection, supported me always not only in the course of this study but in all my endeavors including my tasking political career. He took care of our children and the relatives who stay in Morogoro and in Dar es Salaam. May God bless him and my children Deo, Ami, Neema and Tumaini and relatives. I know this study is another reason for them to go without my care.

TABLE OF CONTENTS

CHAPTER ONE

1.0INTRODUCTION

1.1Background to the study

Tanzania is one of the poorest countries in the world although there is great potential to develop given its rich resource endowment. The country, besides its resources, has been receiving assistance in form of grants and loans both from multilateral and bilateral donors to improve its economic well-being. Yet, forty years of economic struggle have not brought satisfactory progress.

In the meantime, there is substantial consensus among economists that the current economic climate in Tanzania and at most world over is strongly in favor of deregulation, privatization and market oriented economy which entails economic reforms aiming at a different and new economic growth models as well as policies. The new economic models should base on intensified macroeconomic environment; a necessary condition to achieve sustained growth.

While such improvement must be sustained to instill confidence in investors and other economic agents, more effort is needed to bolster complementary structural policies and institutional structures for sustained growth and broad sharing of the benefits that may arise from such growth.

Currently, there is also a deep awareness of the limitations of past development strategies and growing conviction that the way out of present economic crisis of the country does not lie in returning to those strategies which served our country for forty years. The need is therefore increasingly felt for finding a path of development that will lead the country out of the current economic setback, in particular abject poverty, into a future of equitable and sustainable economic growth and development. Fast and sustainable economic growth is inescapable and crucial for Tanzania. A rapidly expanding production of goods and services is the only material basic condition for improving the economic growth path.

Economic growth, essential as it is for creating the resources that can provide the Tanzanian society with better life, is not an assurance by itself of people centered development. The process of economic growth has to be oriented so as to raise the income and productivity of the poor and to promote a sustainable use of the natural resources available. All these require a careful retrospect and modification of the past development strategies.

This increasingly means that previously well protected economy and public enterprises have to adapt their strategies to a newly competitive and unprotected environment, that is to say, environment of trade liberalization. This is indeed the type of climate, which is presently prevailing in Tanzania. The future will probably herald an ever-increasing rate of change in all aspects of economic and business organizational environment. Because future organizations will be more dependent on their environment, performing environment analysis will almost certainly be even more important.

The events that have taken place in the international financial markets, and the predominant tendencies in the international trade environments which are changing more often than not, together with conditions from the international financial institutions, have been determinant factors for the reorientation in regard to most of the domestic economic policies.

These changes that have taken place worldwide have brought about new face in economic growth pattern of these countries. Tanzania already has adopted the market-oriented economy, that is, trade liberalization that has greatly stimulated competition among companies' products of both domestic and foreign origin. The so stimulated competition is gaining more impulse to the extent that it has managed to affect the performance of several organizations. Some of them have closed down since they have failed to compete, while others are still struggling to survive as their performance is less encouraging. Seemingly and more justifiable than ever, we are living in the economic era whereby economic players are struggling for existence and those who are going to survive are the fittest ones. The prevalence of poverty amidst existing competition pressure, limited markets, the cost of making mistakes, and growing citizens, customer expectation all contributed to the need for formulating or adopting a new approach to economic growth.

The immediate task of improving economic growth rate of Tanzania so that poverty is ultimately eradicated is both an economic challenge and a social necessity. What determines economic growth or what the major factors are that drive or hinder higher economic growth has become of much interest among scholars, World Bank and the Government. This study was another initiative to address these specific questions.

Casual observation based on numerous theoretical and empirical studies suggest that investment in physical and human capital, population, international trade, tax policy, Government expenditure, inflation, political stability and income distribution among others have a strong link to economic growth of most countries. To most scholars of economics, these determinants of economic growth provide an empirical analysis of factors affecting the rate of growth in real per Capita-Gross National Product (GNP) (Arrow 1962; Lucas 1988 and Khan et al 1996).

1.2 Statement of the problem

After four decades of independence, Tanzania remains one of the 10 poorest countries in the world (World Bank, 2001). Poverty remains widespread and deep, with half of Tanzanians living under conditions of deprivation. According to World Bank Document (2001), poverty is concentrated in rural areas, where approximately 70 percent of Tanzanians live.

Hitherto, Tanzania mirroring other developing countries embarked on various adjustment programmes from the mid 1980s with the aim of addressing structural rigidities and reducing internal and external imbalances. This is thought to be a quid pro quo for achieving sustainable growth. Many pro-growth policies have so far been implemented aimed at achieving economic growth though the output in actual fact has been dismal. So far the highest economic growth rate of 6.6 percent was recorded in the 1970s declining to negative 2.4 percent in the 1980s, thereafter recovering slowly to about 3.7 percent in late mid 1990s (World Bank, 2000). However to-date the 1970s growth rate of 6.6 percent has not been achieved.

Given the World's and national growing concern over measures to eradicate poverty, a study on the factors affecting economic growth in Tanzania becomes of primary importance. This is in line with the *'trickle down effects'* argument whereby poverty will eventually be combated indirectly.

1.3 Purpose of the study

The review of earlier works indicates that, the determinants of economic growth have been widely investigated in different countries using different variables and models. Most of the earlier works tend to support endogenous growth theories in which development enabling policy environment and capital accumulation especially investment in human capital provides for sustainable long-run economic growth. However, the major shortfall of most of these studies is the fact that they have concentrated much on supply side ignoring partially if not completely the demand side of the growth models. It is in line of this weakness that, this study became of vital importance to undertake.

Moreover, most studies done in Tanzania have focused on investment and economic growth or savings and economic growth or foreign direct investment and economic growth. This implicitly implies that there is no study that has focused solely on economic growth alone. The purpose of this study was therefore to analyze Forty Years of Tanzania Economic performance, growth and development patterns and conditions for sustainable poverty free economic growth.

1.4 Objective of the study

The general objective of this study was to contribute to the design of sustainable poverty free economic growth and development policies in Tanzania.

The specific objectives of this study were:

(i)   To review both theoretical and empirical literature on factors affecting economic growth and development, and to identify major shortfalls that had posed serious setbacks to the economic performance of Tanzania;

(ii) To analyze the patterns in terms of trend of the National Gross Domestic Product (GDP) and Gross National Income (GNI) over the past 40 years of Independence;

(iii) To identify and explain the main causes of economic growth and development in the Tanzania context;

(iv) To determine the conditions for sustainable poverty free and pro-poor economic growth, within the Tanzanian framework; and

(v)   To suggest, based on the findings, strategies for economic growth relevant for the Tanzania context.

1.5 Research questions

The following central research questions were addressed:

(i)   What would be the appropriate investment levels in human and physical capital to attain 8 percent annual economic growth rate in the medium term and 14 percent in the long term?;

(ii)   Could the 25 percent investment rate as sighted in the Vision 2025 that is said to be appropriate in eradicating poverty in Tanzania, be attained?

(iii)   Was high inflation a conducive or hindering factor of economic growth?;

(iv)   What was the extent of tax distortion in Tanzania and how did it affect the economic growth; and

(v)   Was the 2.8 percent population increase in Tanzania appropriate for economic growth?;

(vi)   What lessons could be learned from the above questions about the economic management of Tanzania.

1.6 Significance of the study

So much literature has been written on the factors that determine economic growth. Most studies have focused on growth and investment or savings. However, a major shortfall of all these studies has been that, they have concentrated more on the supply side underscoring the demand side. This is one of the major weaknesses that had been addressed by the study.

A rigorous study on the determinants of growth has contributed to a better understanding of the factors that can bolster economic growth in Tanzania. In face of this, the study has established the contribution of Investment in both Physical and human Capital, International trade, population increase, inflation and tax distortion on the economic growth of Tanzania.

Moreover, the empirical findings of this study would hopefully be of great significance to both economic scholars and policy makers in providing information about the major determinants of growth in Tanzania. This in turn is of assistance in pursuing for better, macroeconomic policies that will disentangle the Tanzanian economy from its long history of poor performance and the surpassing poverty magnitudes.

1.7 The scope of the study

The study covered Tanzania within a period of 40 years. The analysis was based on both qualitative and quantitative evaluation, which is statistical, econometric, and descriptive method. The study made use of various variables that were considered of profound importance. These included investment in both physical and human capital, as proxies for government expenditures in health and education sectors, international trade based on total trade, population growth rate, inflation, and tax distortion.

CHAPTER TWO

2.0 CONTEXT OF THE STUDY

2.1 The country's general background

The United Republic of Tanzania consists of the area formerly known as Tanganyika, which is now mainland Tanzania, and Zanzibar which is made up of the islands of Unguja and Pemba. Tanganyika got its independence from Britain on December 9th 1961 and became a Republic a year later. Zanzibar became independent also from Britain on December 19th 1963 and was named the People's Republic of Zanzibar after the revolution of January 12th 1964. Tanganyika united with Zanzibar on April 26th 1964 to form the United Republic of Tanzania that was ratified by the Parliament on October 29th 1964.

2.1.1 Natural resources endowment

One of the main factors of development of some countries is relative endowment with natural resources. The relative endowments of a country with land, minerals and other factors give it a first impression of its potential for development. This section gives a brief description of the overall picture of potential in natural resources – land, agricultural area, tourism, mining, industry and potential of agricultural exports and potential threats facing the development of some of the natural resources.

Tanzania is endowed with a rich natural resource base and easy access for international trade. It is made up of a total area of 945,000 square kilometers; inland waters occupy 62,000 square kilometers. About 46 percent of its total land area is arable therefore the country has a rich potential for agriculture. With a large hydropower potential and a range of mineral deposits like; gold, diamonds, tin, iron ore, uranium, phosphates, coal, gemstones, nickel, and natural gas deposits, Tanzania has a potential to improve her economy if able to exploit them.

The terrain of the country varies, as does the climate and agro-ecological zones. The terrain consists of plains along the coast, a plateau in the central area, and highlands in the north and south. The vast majority of the population (70 percent) lives in the rural area. Another overriding influence on agricultural potential is the climate, in particular rainfall patterns and amounts especially as the area under irrigation at present is not very significant. The climate varies from tropical along the coast to temperate in the highlands. On average, the country gets an annual rainfall of 1,000 millimeters. The wide diversity in the agro-climatic zones minimizes the countrywide risk of weather related crop failures. Good land and climate notwithstanding, the country has managed, according to recent estimates, to put only 6.7 percent of its land area under cultivation, of which only 1,500 square kilometers is under irrigation and one percent is under permanent crops. The remaining land area of about 40 percent is under permanent pasture, 38 percent is under forests and woodland, and about 15 percent is under other uses.

However, this low use rate camouflages the fact that population densities vary widely in Tanzania, creating pressure on some parts of land, especially in the fertile highlands of northern Tanzania and in the cities. Lack of proper management of land threatens desertification of a sizeable proportion of woodlands in the country. Although the potential of the different Agricultural Economic Zones (AEZs) provides opportunity for diversified agricultural activities, the high dependency ratio may be a hindrance.

It may seem reasonable from the foregoing to conclude that there is enough land for the next 20 years at the current annual population growth rate of 2.8 percent. However, this must be qualified by its impact on the environment without major negative impact on the climate. It follows then that the improvement of land husbandry will have to be addressed so that sustainable land management can be realized. The use of capital-intensive method must be encouraged taking into account the high dependency ratio and migration of the younger generation to urban centers in search of good life.

2.1.2 Income and social development

Despite its potential and rich resource endowment, Tanzania is among the least developed countries in the world. This is mainly because the country is yet to sufficiently and effectively use its potential resource endowment for economic well-being. The estimated trend shows that real growth has been

15

stagnant, resulting into persistent poverty. Tanzania's Gross National Product (GNP) of US$ 265 per capita is low and has increased minimally since 1960 rendering about half of Tanzania's citizens poor. The low incomes have resulted in low average life expectancy at 48 years. Existing data from UNICEF show that the infant mortality rate is 99 per 1,000 live births, and the total fertility rate is 5.5. Only sixty eight percent of Tanzania's population aged 15 years and above is literate.

Although the ratio of gross enrolment in primary school to the total eligible population is officially estimated at 76 percent, the ratio for net enrolment is 56.7 percent. The reason behind being, in Tanzania it takes longer period (an average of 9.4 years instead of the expected 7 years) to complete primary education, another 2.4 years is due to dropouts and repetition, especially at standard 4 level. The gross enrolment ratio in secondary schools is as low as only 5 percent. This low enrolment ratio is based on six years of secondary education.

2.1.3 Demography

In Tanzania, on average, there is no population pressure on land at present. But delayed demographic transition may be a threat to development. It is considered one of the causes of low development. Tanzania has an estimated total population of about 31 million, of whom 30.1 million live on the mainland and about 900,000 live in Zanzibar. The crude birth rate is 41 while death rate is 14 per 1,000 people. There has been a high increase of population over the last four decades from about 9 million in 1960 to 31 million in 1998. On the basis of the latest inter - census data, the current population growth rate is estimated at 2.8 percent, per year. Tanzania's population has a higher proportion in the younger age groups than in the old age groups. The proportion of the total population that is under age 15 is about 47 percent, the proportion between 15 and 64 is 49 percent, and the proportion above age 65 is 4 percent. The median age is 16.4 years, and the dependency ratio rose from 98 in 1967 to 106 in 1996, indicating a rising and unsustainable burden for adults to fend for the dependent population (Economic Research Bureau-ERB, 2000).

The average population density for mainland Tanzania is 34 people per square kilometer. It has increased from that of eight people per square kilometer in 1948. It saves to note that the population density is not uniform throughout the country. According to the 1988 census analysis, population density in the different administrative regions ranged from 9.8 to 976.9 per square kilometer. This variation of population density is even wider, across districts ranging from 1.4 people per square kilometer for one district in Arusha region to 1,579.4 people per square kilometer for another district in the Dar es Salaam administrative region (Census 1988).

The majority of Tanzanians live in the rural area, accounting for 76 percent of the total. The urban population, however, has been rising rapidly as a result of a combination of high population growth and migration from rural to urban areas. Census data indicate that the urban population grew from 6 percent in 1967, to 14 percent in 1978, to 21 percent in 1988, to 24 percent in 1996 and 30 percent in 2000 (Census 1988). As a result, considerable pressure is placed on the limited capacity of urban service amenities and on the growth of opportunities for gainful employment in and around urban centers.

2.1.4 Manpower and employment opportunities

The World Bank Country Report (2000) concludes that because of the high proportion of young people in Tanzania, the labor force is growing rapidly and outstrips growth in employment opportunities. Fifty percent of the labor force is under 30 years old. The urban labor force is 16.8 percent of the total, and the rural area hosts 83.2 percent of the total labor force. The proportion of women in the labor force is 50.2 percent, close to their share in the total population. The rate of growth of the labor force is 3 percent. The number of new entrants into the labor market has been increasing more rapidly than the employment growth rate, and the average age of workers has been declining. Tanzania has about 400,000 to 600,000 new job seekers each year (World Bank, ibid.). The labor force is mostly unskilled and has a low level of education attainment. Only 67 percent of the labor force is functionally literate, 32.1 percent never had any formal education, 21.4 percent went to primary school but never finished, 43.1 percent finished primary education, and 3.2 percent went to secondary school and above.

The statistics given by the Tanzania and the World Bank (2000) on unemployment and underemployment differ greatly. This may emanate from the definition adopted by each. The unemployment rate ranges between 4 and 10.7 percent, depending on the source of analysis. The Tanzanian Government has the total unemployment rate for the population aged 10 years and above at 3.6 percent, with the rate for men at 2.9 percent and for women at 4.2 percent. The Government has the overall underemployment rate at 4.1 percent, 4.3 percent for men and 3.9 percent for women. The World Bank Reports the unemployment rate at 10.7 percent, with men at 9.2 percent and women at 12.3 percent. According to these sources, the overall rate of underemployment is 2.7 percent, with men at 2.72 percent and women at 2.68 percent. Underemployment is most prevalent in rural areas, where labor demand declines seasonally.

Sources indicate that employment grew by between 2 and 3.2 percent during the 1980s and 1990s respectively. The World Bank (2000) reports total employment grew at an annual average rate of 3.2 percent between 1978 and 1988, and continued to grow at the same rate or even faster in the early 1990s. Bank of Tanzania (2001), in contrary, reports employment growing at 2.5 percent during the 1980s with the growth rate slowing to 2 percent in the

1990s. In both cases, the bulk of employment growth was observed to come from traditional agriculture and, increasingly, from the informal sector.

Formal engagement in the civil service, parastatal organizations, and private firms accounts for about 10 percent of the total employment. The Tanzania Government estimates that about 0.81 million people are employed in the formal sector as their main activity, of whom about 60 percent are in the public sector (URT, 2000). While the employment rate is declining in the Public Sector, Private sector employment is becoming more important and has been growing at a faster rate of 10 percent. The number of people employed in the formal private sector doubled between 1984 and 1991 and has possibly declined due to mass retrenchment between 1992 and 1996 after privatization of enterprises owned by the Government.

More than 80 percent of the employed, working-age population is engaged in agriculture. Most of them work on smallholdings as self-employed or unpaid family workers. Those working primarily as paid employees are few, but involvement in casual work is common, especially for youths, women, and members of lower-income households. More and more family members are refusing to work as unpaid family workers and are instead opting to join the wage-earning employment group of the agricultural sector (Mbilinyi, 1993). The informal sector expanded quickly with economic reforms and is considered a growing source of employment, accounting for about 16 percent of the labor force. The Tanzanian Government reports that about one million people are currently engaged in the informal sector as their main activity, and 1.8 million as a secondary activity (URT, 1993). Also one out of four households in mainland Tanzania has at least one person self-employed in the informal sector during the year.

2.2 Economic structure

Results from the study by Kenny and Syrquin (1999) as reported in the World Bank Country Study (2000) depict a very limited structural transformation in Tanzania. The shares of agriculture in total output and employment and of primary exports in total exports trend remained dominant in the total production and exports. The share of investment in Tanzania seems to have risen marginally, from 15 percent in the 1960s to an average of 20 percent in the last five years. The share of food consumption in total consumption has likewise remained stagnant at approximately 70 percent of total household expenditure. Available statistics show the primary exports as a percentage of total exports declined only marginally, from 87 percent in 1965 to 82 percent in 1987. Similarly, the share of the labor force in agriculture decreased from 90 to 84 percent over the same period. Exports as a percentage of Gross Domestic Products (GDP) also declined, from 26 percent in 1965 to 22 percent in 1997. These statistics indicate structural rigidities and hence the backwardness of Tanzanian economy and development.

Agriculture and industry are the mainstays of the economy. Tanzania's economy is mostly agrarian. The economy depends on agriculture, which is predominantly smallholder and subsistence in nature, marked by backward technology and low use of modern inputs. Nevertheless agriculture has significant linkages to other domestic sectors. Agriculture accounts for about 50 percent of GDP, provides 85 percent of merchandise exports (raw and processed), and is directly or indirectly a source of employment and livelihood for 80 percent of the total work force and the majority of Tanzania's. Industry is dominated by the manufacturing sector, which currently accounts for about 8 percent of GDP and concentrates on agricultural processing and the manufacture of light consumer goods. This means that Tanzania has limited production of capital and basic goods. In the past, industrial development strategy pursued was in the form of import substitution which, until recently it has been dominated by public enterprises, and is marked by low technological adaptation and absorption. As competition and the privatization of manufacturing enterprises that formerly were publicly owned gather momentum, signs are appearing of gains in efficiency out of greater use of new technology and proper allocation of resources. Recently, even as inefficient firms folded and the industrial base shrank, the manufacturing sector has maintained growth rates of between 5 and 8 percent. Both industry and commercial agriculture are considered the main bases for modernizing the economy.

Minerals and tourism form a new source for growth. Given the natural and mineral resource endowments of Tanzania, tourism and mining are envisaged to offer a big push toward economic growth. Reports from tourist board indicate that in 1998 tourism contributed 7.6 percent of GDP, up from a mere 1.5 percent in the early 1990s. The sector's annual growth rate has averaged 22 percent over the past three years. The number of tourists visiting Tanzania has increased by 34 percent, from 360,000 in 1997 to 482,000 in 1998. This increase in tourism boosted foreign exchange earnings from the sector by 45 percent, from US$ 392 million in 1997 to

US$ 570 million in 1998. There is tourism policy guiding the sector and much of the business is in the hands of private sector. As much as 25 percent of the land area in Tanzania has been set aside as wildlife and botanical sanctuaries. The country aims to attract more than one million tourists per year by 2010 and raise the tourist sector's contribution to GDP to more than 25 percent. In order for this ambitious target to be realized, more investment will be needed in market research, infrastructure, publicity, promotion, and improvement of service skills.

As regards mining, the opening of the sector to private investment has increased the impetus of Tanzania for the past two years being among the top destinations for mineral prospecting investment in the whole of sub-Saharan Africa, particularly for gold. The government has adopted the Mineral Policy of Tanzania to guide and spearhead the development of the market-oriented approach. This step is also expected to help overcome problems of poor technology and widespread smuggling of minerals. Already there are large entries of Foreign Direct Investment (FDI) in the sector, which hitherto was dominated by artisan and small-scale miners, most of whom used crude mining technology and operated informally. In 1998, the mining sector contributed 1.8 percent of GDP and it has grown to

2.74 percent recently. The target is to raise the contribution of the sector to GDP to 10 percent as new mining operations come into full swing.

2.3 Infrastructure

Infrastructure remains a key constraint to exploiting Tanzania's potential. To achieve the growth and modernization targets described above, Tanzania must pay closer attention to its infrastructure network to enable improved accessibility to productive locations. The existing transport network is geared toward serving an economy dependent on the outside world for output markets and imported inputs, leaving gaps for a cohesive network that would help develop the domestic and continent's market. The vastness of the country and the wide geographical distribution of its economic activities, partly following the location of natural resource endowments, have posed enormous pressures on the rather undeveloped communication and transport systems. Statistics show that Tanzania has a road network consisting of only 85,000 kilometers of roads, of which 10,300 kilometers (12 percent) are trunk roads, 24,700 kilometers (29 percent) are regional roads, and 50,000 kilometers (59 percent) are district roads. District roads include 27,550 kilometers of feeder roads, 20,000 kilometers of district-to-district roads, and 2,450 kilometers of urban roads. Out of the total road network, only about 5 percent are paved and 95 percent are unpaved (10 percent are gravel and 85 percent are earth). Of the unpaved roads, only about 14 percent are in good condition, 25 percent are in fair condition, and the remaining 61 percent are in poor condition. The challenge is therefore to upgrade, rehabilitate, maintain and to expand the road network.

The railways system covers about 3,570 kilometers, with Tanzania-Zambia Railways Authority (TAZARA) railway line covering 970 kilometers and Tanzania Railways Corporation lines covering 2,600 kilometers. Water transport in lakes Tanganyika, Victoria, and Nyasa is not well developed and depends on old vessels. Tanzania has about 123 airports of which only 11 have paved runways. These include the three international airports in Dar es Salaam, Kilimanjaro and Zanzibar.

Much work has been done to improve the communication systems, especially the telephone systems are fairly well developed, but have low coverage across the country and are mainly concentrated in urban centers. This shortfall is partly offset by greater use of radios. At 278 radios per 1,000 people, the use of radios in Tanzania is significantly above the sub-

Saharan African average of 196. Television recently has spread fairly rapidly on the basis of private sector initiative but, again, it is largely concentrated in the five most important urban centers: Dar es Salaam, Mwanza, Arusha, Dodoma and Moshi.

Tanzania has large potential for power generation. Although its hydroelectric power system is relatively well developed by African standards, the cost of power is relatively high and this limits its exploitation. Cost inefficiencies in the distribution system and low revenue collection are the main sources of the relatively high unit cost of power in the country. The electricity supply is dominated by hydroelectric, with fairly good coverage by the National Grid distribution system, which supplies about 85 percent of total electricity. Thermal supply occupies a small proportion. A change from diesel-based to gas-based (using Songo Songo gas reserves) generation of electricity for heating is expected to further lower the overall unit cost of power generation. The current power generation capacity stands at 350 megawatts and is set to increase by another 180 megawatts after the commissioning of the Kihansi hydropower project. In 1996, electricity consumption per capita was estimated at 59 kilowatts. However, power service is concentrated in urban centers and rural electrification is still relatively undeveloped. Solar power is far from being tapped, and areas with no electricity depend solely on other sources of power, mainly firewood and charcoal and to a lesser extent, biogas.

Tanzania is also well endowed with abundant water sources, but the harnessing of this water for irrigation is still inadequate. The installed capacity of water schemes, rated at 1,156,607 cubic meters per day, is still low. Out of this, only about 69.8 percent is fully used. While the overall objective is to provide clean, safe, and adequate water for all by 2002, the current water supply covers only 46 percent of rural areas and about 68 percent of urban centers. Out of the rural coverage, 30 percent is mostly unreliable while 52 percent of the urban coverage is eroded by technical and commercial losses. The formation of urban water authorities is in an attempt to improve supply conditions, urban and rural water schemes are organized into autonomous systems. These urban water authorities are aimed at being self-financing while rural water schemes will still depend on the government subventions.

2.4 Exports

Traditional exports and imports dominate trade, but efforts to diversify are going on. Although recently non-traditional exports are being encouraged, Tanzania's exports remain dominated by primary agricultural commodities. Coffee, cotton, cashew nuts, cloves, tea, tobacco, and sisal have traditionally constituted more than half of the value of total exports. Given the still large share of primary commodity exports, Tanzania's export sector remains highly vulnerable to the vagaries of weather and to fluctuations in world market prices. Non - traditional exports that have good potential in Tanzania include manufactured goods, minerals, services (especially tourism), and horticulture. Non - competitive imports dominated in the past, but competitive imports have increasingly become prominent, creating competitive pressure for more efficient domestic production. This change has brought with it rising cries of protectionism from some local manufactures.

2.5 Reforms

Institutional reforms focus on supporting a transition to a market economy. Tanzania is governed by its 1977 Constitution, as revised in 1984 and 1999. The country is a signatory to the International Human Rights Charter, and its legal system is based on English Common Law, with judicial review of Legislative Acts being limited to matters of interpretation. Power is separated into three branches of government: executive, legislative, and judicial. The country is democratic and adopted a multiparty system in 1992. Elections are held after every five years to elect the President and members of the National Assembly of Tanzania and the President and members of the House of Representatives of Zanzibar. The Presidents' tenure in office is limited by the constitution to two five-year periods. Politically, Tanzania has been stable. The country owes its stability, in part, to a cohesive national identity that is built around a common language, Swahili, despite the country's multiplicity of ethnic groups. The government recently adopted a decentralized governance structure, but it is still predominantly centralized in operation and has weak capacity in terms of public service delivery. To effectively implement market-based economic policies, the government has decided to leave most of the economic activities in the hands of the private sector and concentrate on the core functions of the government. These core functions include; law and order, defense and security, the regulatory framework and the provision of infrastructure.

Over the past four years, the government has embarked on institutionalising market-oriented economic systems after nearly three decades of a socialist approach to economic and social development. For nearly a decade, economic reforms took place against the backdrop of the inertia of the government's control mentality, as well as property rights and legal systems that were designed to facilitate a socialist economy. This disjuncture accounted partly for the lack of a robust private sector response, as possible reversals were feared. Changes in the perceptions of the credibility of reforms needed to be grounded by binding legal and institutional reforms. Recent public service reforms target changes in attitudes and enhanced efficiency in the delivery of public services. Supportive institutions and changes in the legal provisions are needed to buttress the development of the private sector in the economy and remain the main challenges in enabling the economy to move to a higher level of supply response, growth, and poverty reduction.

CHAPTER THREE

3.0 LITERATURE REVIEW

This chapter reviews the theoretical and empirical studies on the basic economic theories of growth. In section 3.1 a general preliminary review on performance of other world economies as well as poverty magnitude is covered. This is followed by sub-section 3.2 which discusses the theoretical framework in economic growth theories. Section 3.3 reviews empirical studies related to the subject of our investigation. Finally a brief evaluation summary on the literature review concludes this chapter.

3.1 General overview

Despite its abundant land and potential in mining and tourism, Tanzania is still one of the poorest by whatever measure used. While natural resources may be necessary for economic growth, they are not sufficient conditions for promoting growth. Literature has shown that natural resources of a country are not consistently correlated with economic growth. Countries with little natural resource base like Japan and Austria have demonstrated this as today they stand out to be among the richest, most powerful economies and fast growing.

On the other hand a country such as Congo with rich natural resource base is among the poorest countries. However, one should not under estimate the role of natural resources in the growth of countries. For example, countries like Saudi Arabia and Soviet Union owe their economic growth to their natural resources mainly minerals and oil. It seems the link between the natural resources and income does not come from population but from population density. In sparsely populated areas like Congo and Tanzania, it is possible to increase income through engaging additional labour into agriculture. In dense population areas engaging more people in agriculture may be a constraint in increasing agricultural productivity.

A good example is when early Spanish colonialists in Latin America turned the large population labour force into productive use in mining and agriculture. Their objective was to export more and import less. This generated surplus that was repatriated to their home country (Furtado, 1976). While there is no consistent correlation between the natural resources endowment with economic growth, as is shown above, there is one between

34

natural resources endowment and population density. There is inverse relationship between population and available land. This relationship is very critical for economies depending on land for livelihood.

Since a large proportion of population lives in the rural areas in Tanzania the land is an important asset in its economic growth and development. With population density of about 37 persons per m^2, Tanzania is still sparsely populated. An apparent problem at present is that, about two thirds of the population is under the age of fifteen years compared to 25% in developed countries. In Germany there are two working age people per one non-working age. Although the abundance of land and potential of the different Agricultural Economic Zones (AEZs) provides opportunity for diversified agricultural activities, the high dependency ratio may be a hindrance to agricultural growth. Another overriding influence on agricultural potential is the climate, in particular rainfall patterns and amounts especially as the area under irrigation at present is not very significant. Economic infrastructure is another hindrance to agricultural growth as it constrains any expansion.

It may seem reasonable from the foregoing to conclude that there is enough land for the next 20 years at the current annual population growth rate of 2.8 percent. However, this must be qualified by its impact on the environment without major negative impact on the climate. It follows that the improvement of land husbandry will have to be addressed so that sustainable land management for the sake of climate can be realised. In exploiting agricultural potential, the use of capital-intensive method must be encouraged taking into account the high dependency ratio and migration of the younger generation to urban centres in search of good life.

3.1.2 Poverty

Poverty is a pervasive word with many definitions. It can be measured by income indicators (World Bank, 2000). It can also be measured by Human Development indices like; literacy rates, health status, life expectancy and other social indicators (UNDP, 2001). However, the most widely used measure of poverty is per capita income. There is strong correlation between the extent of poverty in a country and its GNP per person (World Bank, 2000).

While there is great deal of truth in this proposition, it must be qualified. First, it assumes that the income distribution is even and there is no significant amount of income inequality. For example, in the case of Columbia and South Korea the poverty line was twice as high even though the average incomes of the two countries were the same. Sri Lanka is a low-income country, but its life expectancy was close to that of the industrialized countries. Second, considering changes over time within particular countries, the connection between the growth and poverty reduction, seems to be inconclusive because there is always a fraction of people who may at least be temporarily impoverished.

Because of paucity of data it may not be easy to get accurate figures of the number of people in absolute poverty. What is clear is that different countries have different experiences. The proportion below the poverty line has not apparently fallen. In some fast growing countries like Thailand and slow growing countries like Sri Lanka it has fallen. Third, the association between health or education and economic growth is still not very perfect. World Bank (1990) defines poverty as inability of people to attain a minimum standard of living. The Bank uses per capita income as a measurement of absolute poverty. An income of US $ 370 was used as a poverty line and US $ 275 as those extremely poor. Despite its shortcomings like its arbitrariness and exclusion of other variables (Thirwall, 1994) it is still the widely used measure for inter-country comparisons. Tanzania's per capita income is still below US $ 300 today despite the various development efforts during the period of forty years of independence. Per capita Income measure can also be used in the time series study in Tanzania.

3.2 Theoretical background of growth and development

A number of different relevant theories on growth and development are discussed. These are neoclassical theories of economic growth, classical theory, linear stage theory, international dependence theory, and endogenous growth theory.

3.2.1 Neoclassical theories of economic growth

The theories of economic growth have their origin in the writings of 'neoclassical' economists like Solow and Swan (1956). In their study, a focal point has been the analysis of capacity or potential output of the economy, defined as the output level that is consistent with full employment of capital and labor. The assumptions in the study are based on an attempt to solve the "knife edge" problem posed by Harrod (1939) and Domar (1946) in attempting to attain a balanced equilibrium growth path.

According to the neo-classical growth studies, economic growth is entirely determined by the supply factors and the economy is assumed to be always operating at full employment. In view of this, changes in aggregate demand do not affect capacity utilization whether in the long run or short run.

The empirical study on comparative basis by Kuznet (1963) however, is believed by many economics scholars to be the most elaborate and pioneering work on growth and development. In the study, Kuznet defines a country's economic growth as a long-term rise in capacity to supply increasingly diverse economic goods to its population. This growing capacity is based on advancing technology, institutional adjustment, and ideological adjustment that it demands. He emphasized three principal components in his definition as:

(i) The sustained rise in national output is a manifestation of economic growth, and the ability to provide a wide range of goods is a sign of economic maturity;

(ii) Advancing technology provides the basis or preconditions for continuous economic growth, a necessary but not sufficient condition; and

(iii) To realize the potential for growth inherent in new technology, institutional, attitudinal and ideological adjustment must be made. Technological invention without concomitant social innovation is like a light bulb without electricity; the potential exists, but without the complementary input, nothing will happen.

He was convinced that use of systematic data on economic policies of nations would perhaps permit a more focused analysis of policy reform in developing countries. For him, careful analysis of empirical evidence is the primary basis on which understanding of policy reforms in developing countries can be advanced. In his exhaustive analysis, Kuznet (1993) isolated six main characteristic features manifested in the growth process of almost every developed nation as follows:

(i) High rate of growth of per capita output and low population growth rate;

(ii)   High rates of increase in total factor productivity, especially labour productivity;

(iii)   High rate of structural transformation of the economy;

(iv)   High rate of social and ideological transformation;

(v)   The propensity of economically developed countries to reach out to the rest of the world for markets and raw material; and

(vi)   The limited spread of this economic growth to only a third of the world's population.

The first two features relate to macro economic variables of production and productivity. This suggests that the solution to poverty is economic growth. The third and fourth features relate to structural transformation variables and institutional adjustment to cope with dynamic economic variables one and two. The forth and fifth characteristics relate to the attitude of the developed countries to assist the poor countries.

Kuznet (1963) argues that a faster growth of average incomes is essential to reduce absolute poverty especially in low-income countries where nearly half of the population is actually below the poverty line. As long as incomes are below the poverty line, it is not possible to eliminate poverty until low income level attains or reaches a range of US $ of 700 to 900 when the average income equals the average of the poorest. Beyond this threshold, the incomes of the poorest population tend to grow faster and will be above the average income. Initially, inequality in income is not necessarily a bad thing because it opens new opportunities in the modern sectors. It creates opportunities for higher income. As development process takes place, the traditional sector becomes less important in economic development. This makes manufacturing, commerce and trade to assume greater role in economic development. However, not all countries follow the same process as observed by Kuznet.

A lot of growth depends on incentives and enabling environment provided by the government policy. But one thing is clear; rate of economic growth in low- income countries must be greater than that of developed countries in order to narrow or close the income gap between the developed and poor countries. Growth alone is not enough partly because of the increasing population and partly because of large gap between the average income and income of the poorest segment of the population (Thirlwa II, 1978). He finds solution in a faster rate of economic growth. But he does not provide what is the necessary growth needed to close this gap.

Following Kuznet studies, other findings also agree with his sources of growth. There are two sources of bringing economic growth. First, building a large stock of capital assets and human skills (Tobin, Schlutz, Clark, 1940; Chenery and Taylor, 1968); second source of growth is improving the productivity of these assets and skills (Domar, 1947; Baumol, 1987; Lewis, Ranis and Fei (1961). This involves moving capital and labour between sectors, developing new institutions, inventing, innovation and their adoption. The growth process evolves a continuous change moving towards a higher equilibrium.

Investment and productivity are the key factors in economic growth. This is clearly presented in the most popularized Harrod - Domar growth model. The building block of this model is the assumption that there is equality between savings and investment.

According to the model, savings is defined as a function of income, that is, Saving (S) is some proportion(s) of National Income (y) such that we have a simple equation:

$$S = sY \quad \text{---}$$
(3.1)

Investment (I) is defined as the change in the capital stock K less depreciation. This is denoted as k, and can also be represented by ΔK such that:

$$I = \Delta K \text{---}(3.2)$$

But because the total capital stock, K, bears a direct relationship to total national income on output, Y, as expressed by the capital - output ratio, k, it follows that:

$$K/Y = k$$

Or $\Delta K/\Delta Y = k$ or finally,

$$\Delta K = k\Delta Y \text{---} (3.3)$$

Finally, because total national savings, S, must be equal to total Investment,

$$I$$

we can write this equality as:

$$S = I \text{--}(3.4)$$

But from equation 3.1 we know that:

$S = sY$ and from equation 3.2 and 3.3 we know that:

$$I = \Delta K = k\Delta Y \text{--} (3.5)$$

It therefore follows that we can rewrite the "identify" of saving equaling investment shown by equation 3.4 as:

$$S = sY = k\Delta Y \text{ ---(3.6)}$$

Divide both sides of equation 3.6 first by Y and then by K, we obtain the following equation

$$\Delta Y/Y = s/k \text{ --(3.7)}$$

This is the simplified version of the famous Harrod-Domar equation in the linear stage theory of economic growth. It states that the rate of growth of GNP ($\Delta Y/Y$) is determined jointly by the national savings ratio, s, and the national capital output ratio, k. More specifically it states that the growth rate of national income will be directly or positively related to the savings ratio. This means the more economy is able to save and invest out of given GNP, the greater will be the growth of that GNP and inversely GNP growth is negatively related to the capital output ratio (i.e., the higher k. the lower is $\Delta Y/Y$).

Among others, the basic weaknesses of the Harrod-Domar model include:

(i)   The level of saving required to achieve a target rate of growth may be very different from the levels of savings available when the problem is posed as one of maximizing growth subject to constraints - that is the level of savings necessary to achieve the target rate of growth may conflict with society's wish for present consumption rather than future consumption. The level of savings may not even be achievable because of a limit to the capacity to tax or to "force" saving through inflation. In other words, targets are based on needs and aspirations rather than on the basis of available resources. This is a problem of most poor countries. Hence dependence on external sources for investment.

(ii)   The level of saving required to achieve a target rate of growth may be incompatible with the supplies of skilled labor necessary to work with capital.

(iii) While the model considered the supply side it completely ignored the demand side; that may be a limiting factor in many developing countries. That is failure to expose the goods produced or fetching lower price than the cost of production- A question of availability of market (Effective demand).

Stanlake (1979) gives an alternative model to overcome some inherent weaknesses of Harrod – Domar model. He defines economic growth as increases in the productive capacity over some given time and offers the prospect of reducing poverty without having to make some people worse off. Although by economic growth he referred to a growing capacity to supply, but he could not discuss this subject without reference to changes in aggregate demand. This is because it is no use expanding output if the market for that output is not growing. The problem is then how to ensure that aggregate demand increases at a rate that will just march the growing capacity to produce. If demand is allowed to increase at a faster rate than productive potential, there will be demand inflation. If it grows more slowly there will be unemployed resources. A further problem concerns the stability of the rate of growth of investment as an income-generating force. Investment is seen as a capacity - generating force thus:

(a)   Net investment increases productive capacity

(b)   Increases in investment raise income and demand.

Hence the concept of Marginal Capital-Output Ratio (MCOR)

$MCOR = I/ \Delta O$ -- (3.8)

Where I = rate of net investment

I = an increase in the rate of investment

O= an increase in output resulting from net investment

The lower the marginal capital output ratio the higher the productivity of new investment.

The formula that relates increases in net investment to income is:

$\Delta Y = 1/MPS \times \Delta I = \Delta I/MPS$

The formula tells us by how much income will rise as investment increases:

MCOR = I/ΔO --

(3.9)

I = MCOR X ΔO --

(3.10)

ΔO = I/MCOR --

(3.11)

It becomes possible now to discover by how much investment must increase in anytime period in order to provide the additional income needed to buy the additional output that has been created by the net investment of the previous time period.

To satisfy this condition:

ΔY must be equal to ΔO

i.e. I/MCOR = ΔI/MPS --- (3.12)

MPS is Marginal Propensity to Save.

This is the formula for balanced growth and it can be rearranged as follows:

ΔI/I = MPS/MCOR = <u>Marginal Propensity to Save</u>
Marginal Capital Output Ratio

From the expression above, the implication is that there is a certain level of investment that is needed to make income payments keep in pace with the value of full capacity output.

Investment in physical capital is found to be of vital importance. However, while natural resources may be a stimulant of economic growth, they may not be necessary prerequisites. One of the necessary complementary factors for economic growth is accumulation of physical capital. With low domestic income there is low saving and high reliance on the external sources for investment. A large amount of the external investment is either bilateral or multilateral funding. Evidence from developed countries show labor productivity to be greater than that of developing countries and this is

49

because of capital investment. Equally important, most of the structural changes and innovations require investment in physical capital. However, experiences do differ from one developing country to another. East Asian countries that have a greater output into physical capital seem to have attained a faster rate of economic growth than most of tropical countries like; Tanzania, Ghana and Zambia.

The question is what is the process of arriving at the required growth target to eliminate poverty? Reynolds (1985) argues that the process of economic growth undergoes three chronological phases. First, is an era of extensive growth, followed by turning point, and followed by an era of intensive growth. According to him an era in which population and output are growing without a rise in per capital is usually quite long. For example, in China it lasted six centuries. Analytically, the conventional procedure in which the rate of population growth is simply deducted from the rate of Gross Domestic Product (GDP) growth to arrive at what is defined as net economic growth reduces population growth to secondary importance. Population growth has a role to play in GDP increase (it increases market and labour force). This study looks into the relationship between population growth and economic growth in Tanzania. The relationship expected is negative. However a positive relation supports Reynolds arguments.

3.2.2 Classical theory

Classical theorists like; Adam Smith, David Ricardo, Thomas Malthus & John Stuart Mills all dealt at some length (with some divergent opinion on many issues) with the causes and consequences of economic advancement. For most of them, progress will ultimately end in stagnation. They also believed that free play of market forces would maximize the social good. In the work of technological progress their contentions were unfounded because, by experience, growth and diminishing returns have not been uniformly depressive to the extent of Ricardo and Malthus pessimism. Rising productivity and per capita incomes appear quite compatible with growth of population and the extension of agriculture. Classical development economists greatly under estimated the beneficial role of technical progress and international trade in the development process. There is a definite link between trade and growth, and between technology and growth, issues that this study examined in a bid to establish that link.

3.2.3 Linear stage theory

Rostow`s (1960) linear - stages theory described the transition from underdevelopment to development in terms of steps or stages through which all countries must proceed. This doctrine came at a time when there was no readily available conceptual apparatus with which to analyze the process of economic growth in largely peasant, agrarian societies sometimes characterized by the virtual absence of modern economic structures. Thus, the historical European experience in transforming their economies from poor agricultural subsistence societies to modern industrial giants was used by Rostow in formulating his theory. The logic and simplicity of the utility of massive injection of capital and historical patterns of the now developed country forms the basis of his theory. Hence the linear - stages model emphasizes the crucial role that savings and investment play in promoting sustainable long-term growth. The Harrod-Domar model is used to arrive at appropriate level of investment given the growth rate of the output. Rostow's theory faces a limitation in that stage - making approaches misleading when they succumb to linear conception of history and imply that all economies pass through the same series of stages. Although a particular sequence may correspond broadly to the historical experience of some economies, no single sequence fits the history of all countries. To maintain that every economy always follows the same course of development with a common past and the same future is to over schematize the complex forces of development and give the sequence of stages a generality that is unwarranted. Another approach to the linear stage growth theory includes structural - change and patterns model by Chennery and the change model by Lewis two-sector model.

The empirical research of Chennery and his associates attempted to document precisely how economies undergo structural change while identifying the numeric values. According to Chennery (1960) one can identify certain patterns occurring in almost all countries during the development process despite the variations existing in various countries. He cautions that these patterns may be affected by choice of development policy pursued by the government as well as the international trade and foreign assistance policies of developed countries. According to this model, a correct mix of economic policies will generate beneficial patterns of self-sustained growth. The empirical evidence on the process of structural change suggests that the pace and pattern of development can vary according to both domestic and international factors, many of which lie beyond the control of an individual developing nation.

The Lewis (1954) theory is another structural change thought in nature. His two-sector model of structural change suggests the importance of analyzing the many linkages between traditional agriculture and modern industry. According to Lewis, the underdeveloped economy consists of two sectors:

(i) A traditional, over populated rural subsistence sector without any loss of output; and

(ii) A high productivity modern urban industrial sector into which labor from the subsistence sector is gradually transferred.

The primary focus of the model is on both the process of labor transfer and the growth of output and employment in the modern sector. It followed a certain pattern. Fei and Ranis (1961) argued the process is not automatic. The Lewis model and its modification overlooked the paradox of unemployment in the urban industrial sectors of the Third World. Todaro (1969, 1994) provides a model of labor migration and urban unemployment based on income expectations in towns.

3.2.4 International dependence theory

Because of numerous failures and growing disenchantment with strictly economic theory of development, a different approach was initiated primarily by intellectuals from the Third world. Their approach combined economic and institutional factors into a social system model of international development and underdevelopment. This is the international dependence revolution in development theory.

The international dependence proponents argue that statistical averages that structural change economists calculated from a diverse range of rich and poor countries are not appropriate for comparison. The mere fact that they are averages, are of limited practical value in identifying the critical factors in a particular nation's development process. But, more importantly, diverted attention from the real factors in the global economy that maintain and perpetuate the poverty of third world nations is underrated. This model views the Third World as beset by institutional, political and economic rigidities. These factors emanate from both domestic and international rigidities.

The poor countries find themselves caught up in a dependence and dominance relationship of rich countries. The proponents reject the exclusive emphasis on traditional western economic theories designed to accelerate the growth of GNP as the principal index of development. They question the validity of Lewis' two sector model of modernization and industrialization in light of their questionable assumptions and recent Third World history. They further reject the claims made by Chennery and others that exhibit well-defined empirical patterns of development that should be followed by most poor countries on the periphery of the world economy. They instead place more emphasis on international power imbalance and needed fundamental economic, political, institutional reforms, both domestic and worldwide. In extreme case, they call for outright expropriation of privately owned assets in the expectation that public asset ownership and control will be a more effective means to help eradicate absolute poverty. The argument goes further that government is better placed to provide expanded employment opportunities to ameliorate income inequalities. This approach was expected to raise the levels of living (including health, education, and cultural enrichment) of the masses. The neo- Marxists go even further advocating that economic growth and structural change do not matter.

The thoughts of international dependence theorists alert us of the importance of the structure and workings of the world economy and the many ways in which decisions made in the developed world can affect the lives of millions of people in the developing world. Whether or not these activities are deliberately designed to maintain the Third World in a state of dependence is often beside the point. The fact of their very dependence and their vulnerability to key economic decisions made in the capitals of North America, Western Europe, or Japan, not to mention those made by International Monetary Fund (IMF) and the World Bank (WB), forces them to recognize the validity of many of the propositions of the International dependence school. The same applies to arguments regarding the dualistic structures and the role of elites in the domestic economies of the third world.

Although a good deal of conventional neo-classical economic theory need to be modified to fit the unique social, institutional and structural circumstances of third world nations, there is no doubt that promoting efficient production and distribution through a proper, functioning price system is an integral part of any successful development process. Many of the arguments of the neo-classical counter-revolutionaries, especially those related to the inefficiency of state owned enterprises, the failures of development planning and the harmful effects of growth induced domestic and international price distortion are as well taken as those of dependence and structuralism schools. By contrast, the unquestioned exultation of free markets and open economies along with the universal disparagement of public sector leadership in promoting growth with equity in the third world is open to serious challenges.

Apparently, successful development requires a skilful and judicious balance of market pricing and promotion when market can indeed exist and operate efficiently, along with intelligent and equity oriented government intervention in areas where unfettered market forces would lead to undesirable economic and social outcomes. The majority of thoughtful observers recognize that the most effective way to deal with those diverse social problems is to accelerate the pace of economic growth through domestic and international reforms accompanied by judicious mixture of both public and private economic activity.

3.2.5 Endogenous growth theory

Finally, although still in its formative stage, the new growth theory is contributing to a better theoretical understanding of the divergent long – term growth experiences of developed and developing Worlds by focusing on the principal sources of endogenous economic growth. Though steeped in the neo-classical tradition, these new models modify and expand the assumptions of traditional growth theory to help explain the observed patterns of growth among nations. Whereas the neoclassic model argues that the growth rate tends to be negatively related to the absolute level of per capital GDP, owing to diminishing returns to capital; Solow, (1956) supported by Barro (1991) using empirical findings shows that the endogenous model hold that knowledge driven growth can lead to either constant or even increasing rate of return owing to critical role played by human capital. Empirical work of Barro revealed a positive relationship between education and growth. Perhaps of most important, in addition, they restore a significant role for government policy in promoting long – run growth and development. Examination of the many lessons of this historical growth experience will be made.

In summary, each of these approaches towards understanding growth and ultimately development has something to offer. Their respective contributions will become clearer later when in future we explore in detail both the origins of and solutions to a wider range of problems such as poverty, population growth, unemployment, rural development, international trade, and the environment in Tanzania.

3.3 Empirical studies

A varied number of empirical studies have been carried out in an attempt to examine the main determinants and factors underlying economic growth in different countries. Indeed, as mentioned earlier, many economic variables are considered important for economic growth, including investment, human capital, international trade and inflation. Most economics scholars also concur to the idea that there are certain features, which characterize the underdeveloped economies. These are in most cases identified as absence or shortage of skilled manpower, low savings and investment levels as well as widespread use of unproductive technology, which feature the economies of most of the least developed countries (Chenery and Straut, 1966). In Renelt and Levine's (1992) for instance, a systematic study of numerous economic factors that may account for long run aggregate economic growth, trade and investment are identified as major inputs for growth, though the effect of trade on growth weakens when controlled by investment. According to the study, the initial level of development is found to have a negative effect on growth as the level of human capital conditions it.

Barro (1991) carried a cross-section of 98 countries study on economic growth. In his study, Tanzania was also included covering the period 1960-1985 whereby the study indicated that GDP has a positive relationship with the human capital (proxied by school enrolment rates) and negatively related to the real per capita GDP. Further, the study incorporates the economic variables identified as important stimulants to growth as drawn heavily from the major findings by neo-classical-Swan Solow models. In fact, the study by Barro (1991) accords that of Solow (1956) that growth rate tends to be negatively related to the absolute level of per capita GDP owing to diminishing returns to capital. According to the study, countries with higher human capital have lower fertility rates and higher ratios of physical investment to GDP. The empirical findings also show that growth is inversely related to the share of government consumption in GDP, but insignificantly positively related to the share of public investment. In addition, growth rates are positively related to measures of political stability and inversely related to a proxy for market distortions.

In fact, the implication of such theoretical and empirical results is that, given similar preferences and technologies, poor countries tend to grow faster than rich countries, thus converging toward the same level of income (*the convergence hypothesis as advanced by Solow 1956*). The main reason for this phenomenon in neoclassical growth models is diminishing returns to reproducible capital. Poor countries tend to have low ratios of capital to labor, and consequently have high marginal products of capital. Thus, they tend to grow at relatively high rates.

Experience of some developed and developing countries has shown that higher levels of financial development to be positively associated with faster rates of economic growth (real per capita GDP growth), the rate of physical capital accumulation and improvements in the economic efficiency with which economies employ physical capital. Furthermore, the predetermined component of financial development is robustly correlated with future rates of economic growth, physical capital accumulation and economic efficiency improvements.

Ghura and Hadjumichael (1996) in their study on growth in sub - Saharan Africa carried an investigation on the empirical determinants of per capita economic growth for a large sample of sub-Saharan African countries during 1981-92. Their results indicate that an increase in private investment has relatively large positive impact on per capita growth. Growth is found to be stimulated by public policies that lower the budget deficit in relation to GDP, reduce the rate of inflation, maintain external competitiveness, promote structural reforms, encourage human capital development and slow population growth. The findings also indicate that per capita income converges after controlling human capital development and public policies.

Calamitsis et al. (1999) carried a study on impact of adjustment policies on economic growth. Using a panel data for thirty-two sub-Saharan Africa countries between 1981 and 1997, the study subdivided the 32 countries into four sub-period observations. Among the explanatory variables used was the indicator of human development measured as a sum of index of life expectancy at birth and 1000 less the infant mortality rate. The results showed that for the sample of sub-Saharan nations, the ratio of private investment to GDP as well as human capital was positively and significantly correlated with per capita growth. Population growth is found to lower per capita growth while the coefficients of both human capital and ratio of government investment to GDP has correct signs but insignificant.

Other empirical country specific studies have also been carried out using applications of endogenous growth models. In Asia, for example Tallman and Wang (1994) conducted a country study on the case of human capital and endogenous growth in Taiwan. They observed that, economic development of Taiwan was attributable to the Taiwanese Government's market oriented policies, which placed emphasis on accumulation of human capital in the labor force and increasing its technological capabilities.

In Africa, Ghura (1997) conducted a study on the determinants of economic growth in Cameroon for the period 1963-1996, with special emphasis on endogenous growth and private investment. Like Tallman and Wang's study, Ghura adopted a model, which was a modified version of the Solow-Swan production function. Using Ordinary Least Square (OLS) estimation method, the study estimated two regressions, one with raw labour and another with raw labour augmented by human capital stock. The empirical results showed that human capital development plays an important role in output expansion.

In addition, both public and private investment has a positive impact on economic growth. Further, results indicate that Cameroon economic growth is boosted by economic policies, which creates external competitiveness and prudent fiscal stance.

Beddies (1999) conducted a study on the potential variables that determine economic growth in the Gambia. Using the 1964-1998 data and employing both direct and indirect estimation methods, the empirical results showed that private and government capital stocks as well as augmented human capital had positive and significant effects on the Gambia's economic growth pattern. In addition, the empirical results indicated that the Gambia's aggregate production function exhibited increasing returns to scale, thus supporting the endogenous growth-type model. The study also estimates a series on total factor productivity growth that indicate that Gambia is able to use its resources more efficiently.

Mrema (2001) using the 1968-1998 data for Tanzania carried an empirical investigation on Investment and Endogenous Growth in Tanzania. In the study, Mrema uses private investment, public investment proxied as infrastructural and non-infrastructural investments, and human capital as variables to be estimated. From the study, it is established that real GDP growth is strongly positively related to private investment as well as public investment. However, the study indicated that there was a weak relationship between economic growth and human capital stock. Further, the results indicated that the impact of an increase in the private investment on GDP is positive. According to Mrema (2001), his study findings were consistent with those obtained in other studies done outside Tanzania. In particular, the study showed that the level of development in both physical and human capital accumulation, overall fiscal deficit and structural reforms generally determine economic growth.

3.4 Government economic policy contribution on growth and development

Factors contributing to different patterns of economic growth and development are institutional in nature. One of the central factors is the government influence on the economy. This is done through government policy. Policy is defined as government action and decisions affecting the economic functions. The government actions usually result in gains to some group and losses to others. The decision or action taken differs from one economic system to another. Bognar (1975) identifies two roles of government in economic process. First, the government role is confined to attempts aimed at co-ordinating the resources allocation by giving the priorities. Second, the government is concerned with correcting the economic process started by entrepreneurial decisions and of their political consequences. In turn, in a centrally controlled economy, the most important macro-economic decisions are taken by the power organisation responsible for national economic policy and planning in developing countries.

At the advent of independence and thereafter, the Government of Tanzania, typical to all newly independent governments, felt obliged to improve the welfare of its citizens. In a bid to achieve this goal, the focus has been on issues of policy. In face of this, the expectations have been that the development process would be accelerated. There were many policies initiated and implemented. Policies on nationalisation of the major means of production hitherto in the hands of private entrepreneurs mainly foreigners was perhaps a turning point from the previous policies. Import substitution followed by basic industrial strategy and Universal Primary Education

(UPE) initiated in the 60s and 70s and the current reforms are key in guiding the investment and the growth of the economy.

It is believed that these polices would be reflected on the performance of the economy. All these have had one central objective of spurring sustained economic growth and macroeconomic stability. In 1976, for instance, Tanzania annual investment growth rate reached a record high of 23 percent and it decelerated thereafter dropping to four percent in 1984. The annual economic growth rate also reached its highest rate of 6.6 percent in the history of Tanzania since independence. However, this persistently decelerated to negative 2.4 in 1983 and recovered thereafter to about 3.7 percent in recent years (World Bank, 2000). There are a number of reasons that have been identified to explain this erratic behaviour of growth. Among these include the World Bank argument that low returns on long-term investment have a causal effect on the poor economic performance. However, this might be true for private and commercial lending; it may not be true for bilateral or multilateral lending in the social and directly productive sectors whose rate of return is usually low. The Government contracted these with the low risk associated. The issue of long-term returns could not arise because the risk was already transferred to the public (public debt). The second reason is that, the period after Arusha Declaration was followed by capital flight following nationalisation of major means of production. The political environment was not conducive for private investment. Therefore, one would not consider low returns as the major cause without giving due consideration to the economic and institutional environment governing the business environment.

CHAPTER FOUR

4.0 RESEARCH METHODOLOGY AND MODEL SPECIFICATION

This chapter presents the methodological framework used in the empirical analysis of the study. The chapter is subdivided into six sections. Section one presents the variables used in estimating the growth equation. This is followed by section two which revisits the hypothesis tested in the study. The subsequent section focuses on the time series properties of the data with special attention on testing for unit root of the variables. In section four conceptual framework of the model is presented and discussed. Herein, some of the basic simplifying assumptions of the model are also presented. Section five concentrates on the type and the source of the data used in the analysis. Section six sums up the chapter by briefly discussing the estimation technique used in the study.

4.1 Choice of variables for the study

In estimating the growth equation, the variables, which in this study are considered to have a significant positive or negative impact on economic growth, include: investment in human capital, investment in physical capital, population growth, inflation, tax distortion, and trade and government expenditures. Indeed there are many variables, which in one-way or another influence economic growth, such as money supply, aid flows, debt servicing, etc (Levine and Renet, 1992).

For both technical and logistical reasons, some of these variables have not been included. Such reasons include avoiding estimating over-parameterised model. The other one is to avoid juxtaposing too many variables in a single study that would have been too ambitious. Moreover, different studies have dealt with the impact of say foreign aid on economic growth, Nyauhenga (2001); and impact of money supply on economic growth as well as stability for money demand, etc. Most of these studies have established a strong relationship between the variables and economic growth. In that elucidation therefore, the study avoided repeating and rephrasing some studies that had already been carried out. It is along these lines, that the current study has rescinded some of the variables for analytical purposes. Other variables have continued to grow in importance when it comes to their impact on economic growth. These include variables such as debt servicing which has been claiming a larger share of government expenditures especially in the 1990s. This variable has not been included in our model though it might have adverse effect especially in stifling economic growth because serious debt servicing started just over a decade ago. Such is considered to be a short term especially when one considers the fact that the study covers a period of about 40 years.

4.1.1 Total investment in human capital

Different studies on growth have established a strong positive link between investment in human capital and economic growth. By investment in human capital, the study looks at the extent to which the government expenditure is directed to expenditure in activities aimed at fostering human developmental activities. These include expenditure in education as well as expenditures in health services. Human capital plays a critical role in endogenous growth models, which hold that knowledge driven growth can lead to a constant or even increasing rate of return (Romer, 1990).

4.1.2 Total public investment in physical capital

The general perception backed up by empirical findings as well as various studies is that, increase in physical capital positively impacts economic growth. By physical capital the study consider items like infrastructures, machines, buildings, etc. Thus, increased expenditures in purchase and development of physical capital in Tanzania determines the pace and rate of economic growth. It is therefore postulated in this study that increases in expenditures for investment in physical capital will be positively related to economic growth.

4.1.3 Population

Population growth is another important variable included in our study's equation. Different studies have argued differently with regard to population and economic growth. In this study, it is postulated that population is positively related to economic growth. However one has to be careful on the nature of population that contributes positively to growth. The active population is usually the healthy and physically fit population. A nation with a population dominated by children or elders who are economically dependant cannot benefit from such a population in stirring economic growth efforts. It must also be noted that for a greater period of the study, the economic rate of growth has been lower than the population growth of 2.8. Due to this situation one should not be surprised by the established positive relationship between economic growth and population increase because the economy is highly dependent on subsistence agriculture with little or no mechanization.

4.1.4 Inflation

The theoretical arguments regarding the effects of inflation on growth are sometimes ambivalent. The Tobin-Mundell hypothesis for instance, states that anticipated inflation causes portfolio adjustments that lower the real rate of interest and raise investment and economic growth. One can therefore deduce that higher level of anticipated inflation reduces economic activities, thus lowering investment and growth. Meanwhile, the effect of the inflation level on investment is negligible if the elasticity of inter-temporal substitution is sufficiently small. On average, therefore, high inflation stifles economic growth. In this study however inflation variable may take any sign even though a negative sign would be more expected and reasonable.

Inflation at a certain level may be conducive for growth, however, such conducive level remains to be an empirical question.

4.1.5 Tax distortion

By tax distortion the study implies looking at the pattern of economic growth and revenue performance like the ratio of revenue collection to GDP. In that regard therefore, the postulation is that, tax distortion is negatively related to economic growth. This is however a policy variable and therefore with good policies, it is expected that growth can be achieved through minimizing tax distortions.

4.1.6 Total trade

For long, in the economic growth literature, international trade has been seen as an engine of growth. Most international economists like Ricardo, and Adam Smith argued for international trade as a gateway through to growth. In that regard, therefore, total trade has been incorporated in our growth equation to ascertain its contribution to economic growth in Tanzania. It is postulated that trade will be positively related to economic growth.

4.1.7 Government expenditures

Government expenditures become an important variable in this study because of the limited development of the private sector in most developing countries. The level of government expenditures and the mechanisms through which the expenditure is financed have an adverse effect on the economic performance of any given country. Most development activities depend on governments' development budgets and commitments. It is in realization of this fact, that government expenditure is viewed as an important component in steering economic growth for developing countries like Tanzania and thus its addition in the current study's model.

The expenditure policy through *the cash* budget has somewhat helped the government to achieve the highest level of fiscal austerity ever in the history of the country. To a great extent the policy has helped to overcome the rampant persistent inflation, which had been predominant over the 1970s – 1990s periods. Thus it doesn't put money into the hands of consumers thereby fueling inflation. Government subsidies to inefficient enterprises have been cut off. Medium Term Expenditure Framework and the corresponding institutional monitoring mechanisms are in effect an attempt toward zero – based-budget. Cost sharing measures in social services have promoted people participation and reduced government spending on the social sector, although marginally.

A significant share of government development budget is financed through external sources e.g. grants, loans and credits. The study implies agreement with this in where it acknowledges that "… in 1994 Tanzania was in serious crisis with the donors." Unfortunately, a dummy in the estimation equation does not represent the year 1994. It is worth noting that domestic taxes (represented by the variable Tx) do not affect the portion of government spending (G) financed externally.

The domestic share of development budget has in the past (and even now) been significantly affected (negatively) by foreign debt repayments. Otherwise efforts toward debt cancellation as a strategy toward poverty alleviation would not have been an issue.

4.2 Hypothesis

4.2.1. Testing hypothesis

The problem of statistical hypothesis testing may be stated simply as follows: is a given observation or finding compatible with some stated hypothesis or not? The word compatible as used here means sufficiently close to the hypothesised value so that we do not reject the stated hypothesis. The stated hypothesis is known as the null hypothesis and is denoted by the symbol H_o. The null hypothesis is usually tested against an alternative hypothesis denoted by H_1, which state for example that true $B_1 = 1.5 -$ simple hypothesis, but $H_1: B_2\ 1.5 -$ composite hypothesis.

4.2.2 This thesis hypotheses that:

(i) There is a positive relationship between an increase in both investment in physical and human capital with economic growth;

(ii) Population growth and economic growth drive each other;

(iii) International trade induces economic growth;

(iv) Higher distortionary tax system is detrimental to economic growth; and

(v) High and volatile inflation has a negative effect on growth.

4.2 Time series properties of the data and econometric analysis

The nature of the study under investigation demands the availability of large sample of time series. As mentioned earlier, the data are organized along seven dimensions: (i) GDP growth (ii) Total public investment in human capital (iii) Total public investment in physical capital (iv)Total trade. (v) Population growth (vi) Inflation (vii) Tax distortion.

Prior to actual estimation, some issues relating to the properties of the underlying data have to be addressed. The preliminary tests carried in the study include, analysis of the summary descriptive statistics, correlation coefficient matrix (which is intended to show correlation among variables) and most important the unit root test.

4.2.1 Unit root test

For Econometricians, it is now widely accepted that non-stationary time series data yields inconsistent and spurious econometric results. At present, there are several formal methods of testing for stationarity of time series data. These various methods are refereed to as unit root tests. The most commonly used of these tests are the Dickey-Fuller test and the Phillips-

Perron test for unit root. In developing consistent and reliable non-spurious econometric results, the study carried out the co-integration test, which proceeded as follows: First co-integration was tested for the four variables: the natural logarithms of aid, revenue, general government expenditures and investment expenditures.

Following Engle and Granger (1987) the study adopted the two-step procedure developed therein in testing for co-integration. In testing for stationarity, therefore, the four variables under study utilized both the Dickey-Fuller and Augmented Dickey-Fuller tests. The main idea of the Dickey-Fuller unit root test can be presented as follows: Suppose a process generates the series μ_t:

$$\mu_t = \rho_1 \mu_{t-1} + \varepsilon_t \dots\dots\dots\dots\dots\dots\dots\dots\dots\dots\dots(3.7)$$

Where white noise process generates ε_t. given the fact that ε_t is a white noise, $|\rho| < 1$ guarantees that sequence μ_t is stationary. If $|\rho| = 1$, the μ_t sequence is generated by a non-stationary process. The idea thus to test for stationary time series, is to test for hypothesis that $|\rho| = 1$. However, if $|\rho| = 1$, classical statistical methods of estimating and testing the significance of coefficient ρ_1 becomes inappropriate. In this case OLS estimates of equation above gives a biased estimate of μ_t. The estimates value of μ_t will be biased below its true value of a unit, leading to the estimated model matching a stationary AR (1) process with a near unit root.

To overcome the problem, Dickey Fuller (1979 & 1981) devised a new procedure to test for the presence of a unit root. Equation (3.1) therefore became the starting point for Dickey –Fuller test for unit root. Subtracting μ_{t-1} from both sides of the equation yielding:

$$\Delta\mu_t = \phi_1\mu_{t-1} + \varepsilon_t \dots\dots\dots\dots\dots\dots\dots\dots\dots\dots\dots(3.8)$$

Where the variable of interest, Δ is the difference operator and ε_t is a white noise process. Equation (3.2) therefore tests for negativity of ϕ_1 in the null hypothesis:

H_o: $\phi_1 = 0$ against H_o: $\phi_1 < 0$. If the null hypothesis is rejected and the alternative hypothesis accepted, it implies that $\rho < 1$ and that μ_t is integrated of order zero, that is stationary, implying that μ_t is I (0). If the null hypothesis cannot be rejected, then the μ_t series as a unit root is non-stationary in levels.

So far, one of the major weaknesses with Dickey-Fuller test is that it does not consider the possibility of auto-correlation in the error terms. If ε_t is not white noise, the OLS estimate will not be efficient. The Augmented Dickey

Fuller (ADF) test is used to overcome the problem. The ADF equivalent of

equation (3.2) is presented hereunder;

$$\Delta\mu_t = \rho + \rho_1\mu_{t-1} + \rho_2 T + \sum \alpha_{1i}\Delta\mu_{t-1} + \varepsilon_t \dots\dots\dots\dots\dots(3.9)$$

where T is the time trend and μ_t is the speed of change of either of the

variables under discussion.

Nevertheless, the hypothesis is as in Dickey-Fuller test so that when the null

hypothesis is rejected and the alternative accepted, the series is stationary at

levels. If the null hypothesis cannot be rejected the series are non-stationary

in levels but could be stationary at higher levels or not stationary at all. The

estimation procedure for ADF is more or less similar to DF test.

4.3 Theoretical Foundations of the Model

Numerous theoretical and empirical studies find that human capital,

population growth, trade, government consumption, political stability,

income distribution, inflation and terms of trade determine growth.

Following the Neo-classical growth theories tradition, studies by Barro,

(1991, 1997); Barro & Lee, (1993), Cheng & Feng, (1996) etc, all confirm the so-called conditional convergence of different nations. For instance, Barro (1997) finds that the gap of income per capita between poor and rich nations narrows at a rate of 2-2.5 percent if such factors as education level and the openness of the economy are brought under control. It is along this tradition that the current study moulds its economic growth model under the assumptions prescribed hereunder.

4.3.1 Conceptual framework of the model

Measurement of relationship between variables using a model in economics is essential if one is to describe, explain, and prescribe an economic phenomenon. Measurement in economics involves formulating, estimating and evaluating the relationship between economic variables in question. In the current study, the theoretical framework adopted predicts that investments in human and physical capital contribute to output growth. It is further assumed in the model that, the economy's growth is not static but rather dynamic over time. The model assumes an open economy with human capital utilized only within the economy's territory. In other words, both physical and human capital flight is assumed to be non-existent. In the current study also, public sector is assumed to be relatively larger than the private sector giving much weight to public investment than private investment. Finally the policy climate of the economy under study is assumed to be a pro-growth conducive policy. In that regard therefore, the following growth model is hereby proposed:

Economic growth: $G = f(I, N, T, T_D, \Pi_f, E)$ ....(3.10)

Where G = Economic growth

I = Investment

N = Population

T = International Trade

T_D = Tax Policy

Π_f = Inflation

E = Government Expenditure

The expected signs of the variables in the model are as follows, f'_I, f'_T, f'_N, >0, meanwhile, f'_D and $f'_{\Pi f}$ <0 and f'_E can take any sign because the expenditure policies have not been consistent over a long period of time until when reforms started with attempts to practice fiscal austerity.

The variable on investment is somehow tricky in as much as, under normal circumstance we have public and private investment. However, for a long time, that is, since 1967 with the proclamation of Arusha Declaration, private investment became dismal. At its place public investment took the leading role in almost all sectors of the economy. Public investment continued to dominate the Tanzanian economy until the dawn of economic liberalization in mid 1980s. It is along these lines private investment's contribution to the economic growth in Tanzania under specified period becomes minimal and thus relegated. A focus is therefore on public investment, which is again gauged as a total of public investment in physical capital as well as public investment in human capital. Thus, total investment (I) is a sum of total public physical capital and public investment in human capital, which can mathematically be presented as:

$$I = IP_c + IH_c \dots\dots\dots\dots\dots\dots\dots\dots\dots(3.11)$$

Moreover, total public investment in human capital is further proxied as total government expenditures in education and health services. This can mathematically be presented as:

$$IH_c = TE_d + TE_h \dots\dots\dots\dots\dots\dots\dots(3.12)$$

where TE_d is total government expenditures in education, and TE_h the total government expenditures in health.

To empirically examine these determinants of economic growth of Tanzania, time series data was used. Econometric equation expressing the relationship between economic growth and its determinants was constructed. Estimations were done with the use of regression analysis applying the ordinary least squares (OLS) method. Regression analysis model and co efficient of correlation were of vital use in establishing relation of different variables. The expected relationship is expressed as follows:

$$G = \alpha_0 + \alpha_1 IP_C + \alpha_2 IH_C + \alpha_3 N + \alpha_4 T + \alpha_5 T_D + \alpha_6 \Pi_f + \alpha_7 E + \mu_t \ldots \ldots (3.1 3)$$

Where IP_C = Investment in Physical Capital

IH_C = Investment in Human Capital

N = Population

T = International trade

T_D = Tax distortion

Π_f = Inflation

E = Total government expenditures.

α_i = Coefficients

To summarise the equations, coefficient α_1, α_2 and α_4 are expected to be positive while α_3, α_5 and α_6 negative. The average rate of GDP for the

86

period between 1961 and 2001 was used for economic growth. The average rate of investment in physical and human capital in terms of budgetary expenditure on purchase of machinery and on education over the 40 years will serve as investment on physical and human capital. Average total expenditure on exports and imports over the study time represented the value of Trade, average inflation rates as reported in the annual budgets was used in the model, while proportion of tax to GDP stands for tax distortion and finally average population growth rate was taken as fertility level. The factors that were found to have significant influence were further analysed and those found insignificant were dropped out.

4.4 Data type and sources

Owing to limitation of time, the study mainly made use of secondary data in the analysis. Modern Time series tools of analysis were used in order to arrive at significant determinants of economic growth. The stagnation or decline in the trend of the data was traced for a better result. The primary information on how these variables under estimation affect GDP growth were first sought. In addition consultations with peer groups in the Government were made.

Considering the fact that it is difficult to obtain continuous time series data for the forty years covered under the study period, for the most of the variables, different sources were used to obtain figures that were reliable and quantifiable. In any case, this should not invalidate the consistency and reliability criteria of the data.

Annual series for the GDP growth, investment, trade; inflation rate, population and trade were obtained from different sources. These included: The International Financial Statistics Data Bank, World Development Indicators 2000 Compact Disk - Read Only Memory (CD_ROM), Annual budgets, the Bureau of Statistics and Economic Research Bureau.

Tanzania is taken as a case for study with a belief that meaningful analysis of the growth and patterns of the economy could be traced out. This is because Tanzania has interaction within its borders as well as across, large enough to justify the need for the study.

4.5 Estimation Technique

The study made use of the common Ordinary Least Squares (OLS) estimation technique, which is strengthened by recent development in modern Time Series econometrics. These included testing for Unit root, Jacque Bera Normality Test, testing whether or not, the variables had long run relationships by use of Johansen Maximum likelihood technique of co-integration analysis.

CHAPTER FIVE

5.0 EMPIRICAL RESULTS

5.1 Introduction

This study made use of both quantitative and qualitative methods to examine the factors that determine economic growth. This chapter presents the empirical findings of the study, which is the quantitative part. The chapter is divided into six sections. The current section serves as an introductory part to the chapter. This is followed by section two which focuses on the exploration of the data presenting us with the descriptive statistics of the data used, the correlation matrix as well as the time series properties of the data. Section three concentrates on the estimation of the specified equation, focusing on the results obtained and their interpretations. Moreover in Section four the study presents a brief discussion of the findings on the primary data survey, meanwhile section five carries out a brief comparative analysis with other growth related studies. Section six gives a brief summary of the chapter.

5.2 Data analysis

The properties of the data are ascertained prior to testing the relationship between endogenous and exogenous variables in the study. The results of descriptive data analysis are therefore presented in Table 5.1, which presents all statistical descriptions; meanwhile Table 5.2 presents the variables correlation matrix.

5.2.1 Preliminary problems encountered in the analysis

In the course of analyzing the data used in the study, numerous problems were encountered. In the first place, the exercise on testing for unit root was carried out and all the variables exhibited non-stationarity problem. Most variables were stationary after using lags and were stationary at integration of order one. The total trade variable became stationary only after differencing it twice as Table 5.3 indicates. In the Appendix, some graphs regarding testing for unit root are also presented.

The study also carried out a diagnosis on whether the data exhibited some elements of structural breaks. Instabilities were found to exist for some of the variables in the year 1979, which was the period of Tanzania-Uganda war and also in 1994 as well as 1997. The available information indicates that, in 1994 Tanzania was in serious crisis with the donors who threatened to reduce their assistance to the country because of perceived laxity in revenue collection as well as the excessive corruption that permeated in the country by then. To a great extent, this had an impact on the Tanzanian economy. For the 1997 break, Tanzania was faced with hostile environmental condition whereby the el-nino rains had serious impact on the economy.

In trying to overcome these problems, this particular study attempted to stabilize the data by introducing logarithms as well as differencing some of the variables. In addition, step dummies were used to solve the problem of structural breaks in the final estimated equation. The final equation therefore had two-step dummies for the 1979 and 1997. This partly solved the problem. Following the detected structural break, the study took some trouble to estimating two equations based on the 1979 structural break point. The results obtained can as well be viewed in the Appendix.

5.2.2 Normality Test and Correlation Matrix

Although Ordinary Least Squares (OLS) method does not require normality of the variables, the latter may affect the normality of the resultant residuals. The analysis of the data is therefore important in ascertaining whether they are normally distributed or not. The analysis becomes important owing to the fact that most economic data are usually not normally distributed as they are skewed. This phenomenon is sometimes attributed to the presence of outliers or to the fact that economic data have a clear floor but lack definite ceiling. The absence of normality in the variables mostly impairs the normality of error term and thus affecting the efficiency of estimated parameters. In overcoming such problem transforming the data into logarithm reduces the impact of any outlier in as much as such type of a technique has a bigger effect on large values than on small values.

Table 5.1: The Summary of Common Variables' Descriptive Statistics

	LGDP	LEX	LIMP	LTPI	LTIH	INF	POP	TD	LTGE
Mean	13.346	9.2572	9.9115	9.7147	8.3527	19.260	20.017	0.1084	9.9737
Median	13.768	8.3902	9.1454	8.5943	8.0618	21.000	18.875	0.0518	9.7634
Maximum	14.318	13.028	14.051	13.443	12.318	36.100	33.120	0.4700	14.414
Minimum	8.633	6.9629	6.4676	6.5567	5.2353	1.2000	10.200	0.0020	6.6555
Standard deviation	1.583	2.0612	2.4907	2.2904	2.1515	11.470	7.2875	0.1334	2.3447
Skewness	-2.525	0.7678	0.4019	0.2427	0.2064	-0.1239	0.3640	1.4121	0.2580
Kurtosis	7.678	2.0522	1.7092	1.4918	1.7225	1.5119	1.8317	3.9988	1.8025
Jarque-Bera	78.993	5.292	3.853	3.451	3.003	3.318	3.158	14.956	2.6213
Probability	0.000	0.070	0.145	0.178	0.222	0.190	0.206	0.0005	0.2696
Observations	40	39	40	33	40	35	40	40	37

Key to Abbreviations :

LGDP = log of GDP growth rate,
LTIH = log of total investment in human capital,
LTPI = log of total public investment,
INF = Inflation,
LEX = log of total exports,
LIMP = log of imports,
LTGE = log of total government expenditures,
POP = Population growth,
TD = Tax distortion.

The Jarque Bera normality test reveals that LGDP, LEX, and TD are normally distributed whereas POP, LIMP, LTIH, LTPI, LTGE & INF is not normally distributed at 5 percent level.

In the above data, descriptive analysis did not give either the strength of each variable in the model or the expected sign estimated parameters. It is of primary importance therefore to determine the co-movements between variables in the model. This is carried out by the correlation matrix approach. The interest herein is to obtain the signs and magnitude of the correlation coefficients between various pairs of variables. The computed coefficients and the expected signs are therefore presented in Table 5.2. The inclusion of lags in the estimated equation may affect the sign of coefficients. The correlation matrix is an important indicator, testing the linear relationship among variables. The matrix also indicates the strength of the variables in the specified model. One important implication that can be deduced from the correlation matrix in Table 5.2 is the fact that most of the pair-wise correlations among variables that appear as regressors in the equation are low. This implies that the estimated equation containing these variables do not therefore suffer from serious multicollinearity as well as heteroscedasticity problems.

Table 5.2: Correlation Matrix

	LGDP	LEX	LIMP	LTPI	LTIH	INF	POP	TD	LTGE
LGDP	1	0.957	0.975	0.979	0.977	0.499	0.985	0.701	0.984
LEX	0.957	1	0.989	0.984	0.955	0.329	0.973	0.814	0.967
LIMP	0.975	0.989	1	0.995	0.983	0.419	0.982	0.756	0.983
LTPI	0.979	0.984	0.995	1	0.982	0.426	0.983	0.746	0.982
LTIH	0.977	0.955	0.983	0.982	1	0.497	0.972	0.669	0.976
INF	0.499	0.329	0.419	0.426	0.497	1	0.439	-0.107	0.459
POP	0.985	0.973	0.982	0.983	0.972	0.439	1	0.774	0.994
TD	0.701	0.814	0.756	0.746	0.669	-0.107	0.774	1	0.750
LTGE	0.984	0.967	0.983	0.982	0.976	0.459	0.9948	0.750	1

From the correlation matrix, with the exception of inflation (INF) and tax distortion (TD), which are negatively correlated, all other variables, were positively correlated as they all bear positive signs. Surprisingly, the correlation matrix suggests that inflation and tax distortions are positively related to economic growth. Under normal circumstance this does not make sense and it makes it difficult to rationally explain. This could however be explained by inconsistency in the data compilation as the data were computed from various sources.

5.2.3 Testing for Unit Root

This subsection provides the results of the order of integration for each of the variables. The unit root tests were performed using the Augmented Dickey Fuller (ADF) tests whose general equation is specified hereunder:

$$\Delta X_t = \beta_{1j} + \beta_{2j} X_{t-j} + \beta_{3j} T + \sum_{i=1}^{k} \beta_{4j} \Delta X_{t-1} + \mu_t \dots \dots (5.1)$$

for X_t= LGDP, LTIH, LTPI, POP, LTT, TD and INF, T= trend, β_{1j} are coefficients with β_{2j} representing the coefficient used in the unit root test. The null hypothesis is that $\beta_{2j} = 0$ (that there is a unit root) against the alternative hypothesis that $\beta_{2j} < 0$ (implying that the variable is stationary).

The results of the unit root test are presented in the Table 5.3 using different versions of the ADF equation specified above (some graphs are attached in the Appendix).

Table 5.3: Unit Root Test for the Variables

Variable	Nature of Selected ADF Equation	ADF Test Statistic	Order of Integration
LGDP	1 lag	-4.5522**	I (1)
LTPI	0 lag	-4.6107**	I (1)
LTIH	0 lag	-4.8551**	I (1)
LTGE	2 lags	5.5584**	I(0)
LEX	2lags	-1.8131*	I(1)
TD	1 lags	-2.3182*	I (1)
LIMP	1 lag	5.5584**	I(0)
INF	2 lags	-4.8433**	I (1)
POP	0 lag	-4.2981**	I (2)

Notes: ** and * means that the differenced equation is stationary at the one percent and five percent level of significance respectively. The ADF statistics presented here were for the final stationary process (i.e. after differencing) except for the LGDP.

5.3 Estimation results and interpretation

In this section, the study reports the econometric results obtained from the secondary data on the determinants of economic growth for the case of Tanzania. Economic growth is regressed as endogenous variable whereas investment in human capital, total investment in physical infrastructures, growth in population, growth in total trade, inflation and tax distortion are exogenous variables.

The procedure of estimation used has been elaborated in the previous chapter on methodology. The study by use of Ordinary Least Squares (OLS) method estimates equation (4.2) presented in chapter four. The results obtained for the estimated equation are presented hereunder.

Table: **5.4 Results of Modeling Economic Growth by OLS**

Dependent Variable: LGDP
Method: Least Squares
Included observations: 32 after adjusting endpoints

Variable	Coefficient	Standard Error	t-Statistic	Probability.
C	12.96155	0.128029	101.2389	0.0000
LTPI	0.037859	0.037592	1.007108	0.0008
LTIH	0.015191	0.042625	0.356380	0.0250
LEX	0.007717	0.041178	0.187409	0.0031
LIMP	-0.025260	0.055855	-0.452249	0.6555
POP	0.029157	0.015636	1.864721	0.0756
TD	-0.248973	0.169958	-1.464910	0.1571
INF	0.000375	0.001190	0.314992	0.7557
LTGE	0.000536	0.036888	0.014522	0.1085
DUM94	0.019333	0.060670	0.318651	0.7530

R-squared	0.983645	Mean dependent var.	13.89265
Adjusted R-squared	0.976954	S.D. dependent var.	0.242891
Standard error of regression	0.036873	Akaike info criterion	-3.512359
Sum squared resid.	0.029912	Schwarz criterion	-3.054317
Log likelihood	66.19774	F-statistic	147.0140
Durbin-Watson stat	1.737435	Prob. (F-statistic)	0.000000

Key to Abbreviations:
All variables starting with L are estimated in logarithmic form.
LTPI   = Log of total public investment,
LTIH   = Log of total investment in human capital,

98

POP	= population,
LTT	= Log of total trade,
INF	= Inflation,
TD	= Tax distortion proxy of tax revenue to GDP ratios,
DUM1979	= Step dummy for the year 1979, and
DUM1997	= Step dummy for the year 1997.

The representation of the estimated equation can therefore be presented as follows.

Estimation Equation:

LGDP = C (1) + C (2)*LTPI + C (3)*LTIH + C (4)*LEX + C (5)*LIMP + C (6)*POP + C (7)*INF + C (8)*TD + C (9)*LTGE + C (10)*DUM1994

Substituted Coefficients:
=====================
LGDP = 12.96155 + 0.037859*LTPI + 0.015191*LTIH +0.007717*LEX-
0.025260*LIMP + 0.029157*POP +0.000375 *INF - 0.248973*TD +
0.000536*LTGE +0.019333*DUM1994

Following our estimation results above, the model has a good fit ($R^2 = 0.98$). The fact that investment in physical capital, human capital, exports and population were significant at 5 percent level indicates that the variables were indeed important in explaining economic growth.

However, contrary to earlier stated hypothesis in chapter one as well as in the methodology, inflation had an unexpected positive sign i.e. a rise in the level of inflation was positively related to GDP growth However, the subtle findings finds consolation in the fact that the strength of the variable was not very significant. In fact, this could be explained by the question of data inconsistency as well as structural breaks, which were exhibited in the analysis of the data as mentioned above. However, minimum inflation is argued for as a stimulant to demand as well as economic growth. Surprisingly, as opposed to the hypothesis, total trade which in the model has been disaggregated to exports and imports bore very interesting signs. Exports had a positive sign whereas imports had a negative sign. This could be explained by the fact that most of the imported goods were not pro-growth goods as they were just consumables which sometimes acted as linkages to the economy's scarce foreign currency. The use of exports and imports variables in place of total volume of trade is debatable, as other variables such as openness of the economy could as well have been used. The probability is that the use of other proxy such as the openness of the economy, which is usually exports plus imports divided by GDP, would have been more appropriate. Moreover, another explanation was that the nature and type of goods the country dealt with in import/export business

100

had to be revisited. This could as well prove to be difficult because of the forces of globalization, which demanded all countries to liberalize trade.

The Wald Test for the significance of the imports variable in explaining the study's growth equation was also not very high as Table 5.5 shows.

Table: 5.5 Wald Test for LIMP

Null Hypothesis:	C (5)=0		
F-statistic	0.163991	Probability	0.688586
Chi-square	0.163991	Probability	0.685508

From Table 5.5, the Wald Test for LTT indicates that the relative importance of the variable was not very high as the significance level was minimal and thus making it a very poor determinant of growth in our equation. This could as well be the reason why it had taken a negative value contrary to the study's expectation.

The results obtained also showed that total investment in human capital (LTIH) coefficient was very small even though its significance was around 1 percent. This called for a serious reconsideration of the amount of budget allocated for investing in human capital, as one would expect that investment in human capital contribute significantly into economic growth.

Indeed, the total amount of budgetary allocation spent in human capital was a fractional proportion of the total national income. It is also true that human capital takes long to show impact on GDP growth.

For the total public investment, the results were astounding as the variable itself was highly significant whereas the coefficient was small. The Wald Test, however, which tests for the relative importance of the variable in the specified equation for the two variables, that is total investment in human capital (LTIH) and total public investment (LTPI), showed that both variables were important in the model as Tables 5.6 and 5.7 indicate.

Table: 5.6 Wald Test For LTPI

Null Hypothesis:	C (2)=0		
F-statistic	820.1643	Probability	0.000000
Chi-square	820.1643	Probability	0.000000

The Wald Test for total public investment above showed that the relative importance of total public investment in the specified equation was significant at 100 percent in explaining economic growth equation, as the F-statistic and Chi-square probabilities indicate.

Table: **5.7 Wald Test for LTIH**

Null Hypothesis:	C (3)=0		
F-statistic	5.346388	Probability	0.027810
Chi-square	5.346388	Probability	0.020765

Table 5.7 shows the significance of total investment in human capital in the specified model. The relative importance of this variable to explaining economic growth in the specified model was significant at 5 percent as the F-statistic probability indicated. Moreover, other variables explaining the growth equation had relative importance with the average significance level of 5 to 10 percent.

5.4.1 Summary of the findings

From the results in section 5.4, it is observed that economic growth was determined by investment in human capital, total public investment, and population growth. Export trade also determined growth, whereas imports played a detrimental role on economic growth. Meanwhile, tax distortion also had a significant negative impact on economic growth of Tanzanian economy. Nevertheless, inflation, which according to the hypothesis of this study was supposed to have a negative sign, exhibited instead a positive sign even though its significance was very low as its probability value was very low. The explanation of this particular finding is a tricky one, as it would mean advocating for high inflation in order to impact economic growth. This study did not of course take that line of argument and instead, it was believed that the positive sign borne by the inflation variable could have arisen from lack of consistency in the compilation of the data used in the study.

It is worth noting however, that the significance of total investment in human capital and total public investment was relatively high as it reached around 1 percent but the coefficient itself was very low. This could be partly due to small share of GDP ratio to expenditures in these sectors. Meanwhile, the studies show that a higher distortionary tax rate will stifle economic growth.

Moreover, it is worth mentioning that, after failing to obtain the expected coefficient sign of some variables as hypothesized earlier, this study attempted to disaggregate the total trade variable and estimated an equation with exports and imports as separate variables as expected. The results were that the coefficient for exports variable had a positive sign whereas, that of imports had a negative sign. Meanwhile, inflation coefficient continued to bear a positive sign though with less significance.

For curiosity purposes, the study endeavored to estimate two separate equations based on the 1979 predicted structural break and the results were not very impressive. These are found in the Appendix of the study. Other estimated equations that did not bear very impressive results are also attached in the Appendix.

5.5 Comparing the study findings with other studies in the literature

This study bears some resemblance with some of the previous studies done in this area but it is also distinctive as it has some basic uniqueness. The study tried to bridge the gap between the traditional neo-classical growth theories and the recently developed endogenous growth theories.

In the traditional growth theories, the investment component is always seen as a key variable that determines economic growth. Other variables in that line include savings, government expenditures, trade and consumption. In this study, investment in physical capital, government expenditures and trade were included. The findings suggest a strong relationship between investment in physical capital and economic growth. Government expenditure also, though less significant with small coefficient value was also found to be positively related to economic growth and thus confirming the previous study findings.

In the recent developed endogenous growth theories, investment in human capital research and development are incorporated as key variables determining the speed and pace with which an economy grows. In this study, from both theoretical backgrounds and empirical findings all variables were seen as important and key determinants of growth. Investment in physical capital and trade especially on exports was found to be significant components of growth. Indeed this is in conformity with the Neoclassical approach to growth (Solow, 1956).

The empirical work by Barro (1991) reveals a positive and very strong relationship between education and economic growth. In his study, Barro (1991) used school enrolment rates as a proxy to investment in human capital. In this study, this was also confirmed as investment in human capital represented by public expenditures in health and education was significantly found to be positively related to economic growth.

The study by Mrema (2001), which established a strong positive relationship between GDP growth, private as well as public physical investment in Tanzania is also partly in conformity with this study's findings. Other studies done in China by Baizhu Chen, et al (2000) investigating the determinants of economic growth in China identified more or less the same variables as one used in this study and were found to be highly significant in determining the economic growth of China.

CHAPTER SIX

6.0 SUMMARY, CONCLUSIONS AND RECOMMENDATIONS

6.1 Introduction

This chapter presents the major conclusions that the study has come out with. The chapter is subdivided into five sections whereby the current one serves as an introductory section to the chapter. Section two summarizes the study's major findings subsequently followed by Section three which is based on the policy recommendations of the study. Section four presents the major limitations of the study, while Section five identifies new avenues of further research on the topic of growth for the Tanzanian economy.

6.2 Summary of the study

In the current study, basing on both theoretical and empirical foundations, attempts were made to analyze the most fundamental variables that influence economic growth for the case of Tanzania over the past 40 years of independence. This study presents us with the background information on Tanzania economic, political, geographical and social situation. The background knowledge on the situation of Tanzania has helped in the choice of variables thought to have considerable contribution in economic growth and development of the country. Such knowledge is thought to be of fundamental importance in charting out solutions to abate poverty.

From the study's empirical analysis, the selected variables showed that to a greater extent, population rise, tax distortion, inflation and exports and to a lesser extent investment in human and physical capital as well as imports were important in explaining Tanzania's economic growth. It is however, important and worth mentioning that the ultimate goal of the current study was to dig into the policy implication of these variables in relation to poverty eradication. Hence in this chapter policy recommendations are given.

According to the empirical analysis, the findings showed that both investments in physical, capital and human capital were important and positively related to growth. Their significance though differs as investment in total public physical investment was significant at almost 100 percent, whereas that on public investment in human capital, the proxy of public expenditure in health and education, was significant at around 5 percent. Moreover, the disaggregated total trade showed that export variable was positively related to growth at about 1 percent level of significance, even though the coefficient seemed to be small.

This study therefore advocates for a larger share of government expenditure in human capital as well as public physical investments. It is believed that such investments would have a much higher impact on growth if they constitute a lager GDP/ expenditure ratios. Human capital is essentially critical for less developed countries as this would lead to higher output growth which, in turn, results in still greater physical and human capital accumulation.

Furthermore, population growth was also positively related to economic growth at about 10 percent level of significance. This implied that population was still one of the important variables conducive for economic growth in Tanzania even though there had been various campaigns to population reduction. In Tanzania the dependency ratio, as explained before, is high. Thus the study has established a positive relationship between population growth and economic growth only for the case of economically and physically active population. With the case of inflation, it was surprisingly found to be positively related to economic growth but its significance level and even the coefficient remained to be very low or rather extremely small. This could be explained by shortfall in the data used.

Policy variables such as tax distortion have a negative impact on economic growth. This, in other words, suggest that government should exercise prudent tax laws that would in turn contribute positively to economic growth. Moreover, export trade is strongly to be encouraged as it acts as an engine of growth. The negative sign of trade in imports on economic growth is expected. This calls for a prudent import exercise especially on the nature and type of imported goods. This may prove tricky and difficult to achieve especially in our globalized world. Thus, as already pointed out, if most of these are consumables, which do not contribute to physical investment and other sectors that have positive impact on economic growth, then the nation has to adjust and adopt a more friendly importing goods policy.

Due to resource limitation the study could not exhaust all variables, which contribute to economic growth and development of the country. Variables like monetary policy, government expenditure policy and tax policy have had significant effects on Tanzania's economy, though, in the later years of

1990s. A brief observation on these variables forms the last part of this chapter.

6.3 Policy implications and recommendations of the study

As explained earlier, the findings of this study showed that population rise had a positive contribution to economic growth. The implication of this finding is that, population planning must take cognizant of this fact. The Harrod-Domar type model support the findings and their is one classic example reading 'in Golden state "natural" growth rate of population equal the "natural' growth rate in per capital income'.

In Tanzania like in other small agrarian economies, agriculture employs over 70 percent of the population. With land available for expanding agricultural activities, population increases are more likely to be followed by increases in land under agriculture. Besides, population rise is also needed in expanding markets for industrial production. It is however important that the population rise must be accompanied by modernization of the economy especially agricultural production. This is essential as the dependency ratio is quite high in Tanzania. Agricultural mechanization must be given the priority it deserves.

The population issue is sometimes a delicate one especially owing to the fact that the demographic structure of Tanzania's population indicates that the country suffers from a high dependency ratio. Most of the population belongs to the unproductive category of young children between 1-18 years. This, to a great extent, explains high degree of child abuse, i.e., child labor, as productive population does not meet the demands. Again, the HIV/AIDS pandemic to a large extent is affecting skilled people of the nation and continues to affect the majority of the productive population. This in a way calls for serious reconsideration of the status of the nation's population and its contribution to economic growth as well as poverty reduction efforts.

The positive sign of inflation shown by the result of the study was quite unexpected because inflation is never healthy in any economy. Nevertheless, according to Tobin's Model (1972) supposition, that money supply is neutral, does in part explain the positive relationship of inflation to economic growth. Non-neutrality of money is also applicable in the Tanzanian economic context.

In Tanzania, inflation started an upward path in 1973 at 11 percent and maintaining an average of 30 percent up to 1995, and an average of 16 percent between 1995 and 1998; that is a total of 25 years of sustained high inflation of 20 percent to 30 percent per annum. It is also during this time that Tanzania's economic growth reached its peak of 6.6 percent. It follows that the reality in the past has not supported negative sign.

A monetary definition of inflation is a sustained upward trend in the level of prices. This implies that it may be difficult to detect inflation because:

(i)   Not all upward movements of price level are inflationary. Upward prices may reflect adjustments in demand and supply e.g. in periods of poor harvest (low or no rains);

(ii)   Calculations of price indices in Tanzania, especially consumer price index, weigh heavily in agricultural products. The composite consumer price index is about 60 percent based on agricultural products prices Bank of Tanzania Annual Report 2000); and

(iii)   There is a possibility that growth of price level was faster than growth of level of money supply implying money national income was increasing while output was declining at slower rate than inflation rate.

In line with the foregoing explanation, Bank of Tanzania needs to look into the products basket in determining inflation. To attract investors in the country, downward inflationary trend must be maintained to assure them of cheap supplies and effective markets for their products. Since it is through the control of money supply that low inflation was attained, the Government must put in place policies that will lead to more production of goods. This entails the use of country's reserve in bringing down the interest rate without jeopardizing the national economic strength.

Regarding investment in Human Capital, no country can develop without investing in its future. Although it takes time to realize benefits of investing in human capital, it is a worthy investment especially in the absorption and utilization of new and modern technology. The Government is urged to increase expenditure in education and health to reach the critical level to ensure the contribution of its human resource to growth and development.

Trade is one of the determinants of development and modernization. Since time immemorial, nations have depended on trade for development. Unfortunately, in the Tanzanian situation, net outflows of trade have far exceeded net inflows during the period under study. This has forced the country to finance much of its development activities through borrowing. To reverse this trend, exports both in terms of quantity and quality need to be increased. To achieve this, Tanzania must diversify its exports from the traditional primary products to tourist trade, mining and fish products. Instead of exporting raw products, efforts must be made to add value through processing of agricultural products before they are exported.

It is also important to concentrate on growth of friendly imports. The money obtained from trade must be pumped into agricultural modernization to improve its productivity. As agricultural productivity increases, labor and other resources saved should be directed to industrial development.

As considerable tax distortion was observed and that it affects economic growth negatively, to-date tax collection ratio to GDP is below 12 percent. Considering the low income of the country, the tax collection hardly finances even current expenditures of the government. The crux of the situation lies in the low-income generation capacity of the nation. In order to improve such low capacity in agriculture, industry and other economic activities, production in these sectors must be increased. This must be accompanied by prudent tax policy, which will lead to widening the tax base and increasing the collection efficiency.

116

On the government expenditure front, it is observed to be positively related to economic growth even though its significance is not very high and the coefficient is also small. However, government expenditure appear to be a pro-growth expenditure implying that increasing government expenditures will lead to higher economic growth. This indeed has to be practiced with caution as sometimes government expenditures may stifle growth especially when it involves printing money or "crowding out" the private sector. Moreover, government expenditures have to give sectoral priority otherwise it may prove to be a futile activity especially when general government consumption is higher than development expenditures. Expenditures become pro growth when it gives priority to development sectors such as infrastructures, human capital development, etc.

6.3.1 Revisiting the research questions

In attempting to answer the research questions, the study has come out with the conclusion that, given the variables' contribution to growth, the 8 percent economic growth will be achieved only if investment in physical capital is increased by 21.1 percent whereas public investment in human capital has to be increased at least by 52.6 percent.

About the population growth, clearly the 2.8 percent growth rate is not enough to meet the 8 percent economic growth target. Implicitly the study would suggest a relatively higher population growth rate. However, rather than suggesting increase in population, a plausible alternative would be mechanization of agriculture in order to increase the productivity of the agricultural labour force, as well as starting up agro-processing industries in a bid to increase value added to agricultural exports.

In some way, the 25 percent growth rate as envisaged in the Government of Tanzania vision 2025 may not be achieved under the prevailing circumstance as the empirical findings does not really seem to support the hypothesis. However, it is important for necessary adjustments to be carried out in time, early enough to increase the likelihood of achieving the fore stated objectives.

6.4 Limitations of the Study

Due to limitation in time and difficulty in obtaining the required data, some variables such as money supply and monetary policy, foreign aid flows etc., which have had significant effects on Tanzania's economy since 1990, were not considered. It is the expectation of this study that if such variables were considered, the likelihood of obtaining slightly better results could be high.

The study was also limited in the data as only secondary data were used for analysis whereas the primary data were not incorporated in the study. Because of this limitation, some of the empirical findings were somehow unrealistic as most of the data were missing. Data collection, storage and consistency for most developing countries is a heartbreaking problem and this in someway limited the findings of the current study. However this does not nullify some fundamental findings of the study, as the conclusions remain valid and worthwhile considering.

6.5 Areas for further research

As earlier reported, three variables namely monetary policy, Government expenditure policy and tax policy have had significant effects on Tanzania economy especially starting from 1990. If time permitted the model framework, which formed the basis of model specification, identification and subsequent results of the study is to include the three named variables. It is therefore suggested that future research studies should consider using them to construct a model in determining their contribution to economic growth and development guided by thought given below or otherwise.

Monetary policy: Open market operations meant to contain inflation rate through siphoning money from people's hands. It has succeeded tremendously in lowering inflation from 36 percent (1990) to 6 percent (2000). While impacting on inflation rate, open market operations (monetary policy) have not significantly affected interest rates. This implies little effect of monetary policy on investment in as long as interest rate affects investment. There are three instruments of monetary policy: open market operations, changes in reserve requirements and changes in discount rates. All the three affect Bank reserves ability to lend. Thus, they are considered as single tool of monetary policy since they are not independent. Reserve requirements ratio and discount rate changed once after 1991. Open market operations have been practiced on a weekly basis since then.

Another interesting area for research is one on impact of foreign aid and debt servicing on economic growth. Aid servicing has proved to be a leakage to growth because it does not contribute in any way to economic growth as it just services the debt, which in one way seem to be a kind of a deadweight loss to the nation. An empirical study in this area would yield interesting findings. Some studies have been carried on impact of foreign aid on economic growth but none of these studies have looked into debt servicing category and its impact on economic growth.

BIBLIOGRAPHY

Amartya S. (1970) "Growth Economics." Battimore, Penguin Books.

Arrow, K.J. (1962) "The Economic Implication of the Learning by Doing" *Review of Economic Studies,* Vol.9, pp.155 - 73.

Bank of Tanzania, (2001) Monthly Economic Review, ISSN 0856 - 6844.

Bank of Tanzania (2000) "Economic Bulletin for the quarter ended 31 Dec.2000". Dar es Salaam, Bank of Tanzania.

Baran, P.A (1968) "The Political Economy of Growth." New York, Modern Reader Paper-Backs.

Barro, R.J. (1991) "Economic Growth in Cross-Section of Countries." *The Quarterly Journal of Economics,* Vol. 106, pp.407-44.

Baumol, W.J., B.B. Sue Anne et al (1989) "Economic Theory and operation analysis, 4th Edition." New Delhi, Prentice Hall of India.

Beddies, C.H. (1999) "Investment, Capital Accumulation and Growth." Evidence from the Gambia, *International Monetary Fund Working Paper. No. 51.*

Bognar, J. (1975) "Economic Policy and Planning in Developing Countries." Budapest, Academia Kiado.

Calamitsis, E., A. Basu, and D. Ghura (1999) "Adjustment and Growth in sub-Saharan Africa." *International Monetary Fund Working Paper No.51.*

Chenery, H.B. and L. Taylor (1968) "Development Patterns Among Countries and Overtime." Review of Economics and Statistics.

Chenery, H. (1960) " Pattern of Industrial Growth." *American Economic Review, Vol. 50.*

Cliffe, L., J.S. Savl (1973) "Socialism in Tanzania." Vol. 2, Policies. An Inter Disciplinary Reader, Dar es Salaam, East African Publishing House.

Domar, R. (1939) "An Essay in Dynamic Theory" *Economic Journal Vol.4, pp.43-59.*

Fisher, A.G.B (1939) "Production": Primary, Secondary, and Tertiary Economic Record.

Ghura, D. and M.T. Hadjimichael (1996) "Growth in Sub-Saharan Africa." *International Monetary Fund, Staff Papers.* Vol. 43, pp. 605-34.

Furtado, C. (1964) "Development and Underdevelopment." Berkeley, California University Press.

Furtado, C. (1976) "Economic Development of Latin America", Cambridge, Cambridge University Press.

Gracker, C.W.J. (Ed.) (1990) "Modeling Economic Series: Advanced Texts in Econometrics". Oxford, Clarendon Press.

Gregory, S. (1980) "Comparative Economic Systems." Boston, Houghton Mifflin Company.

Hayman, D.N. (1989)"Macro-Economics." Boston, Irwin.

International Labor Review (1971) "Income Expectations, Rural Urban Migration and Employment in Africa." Geneva, ILO.

Khan, M. and C. Reinhart (1990) "Private Investment and Economic Growth in Developing Countries." *World Development Report*, Vol. 18, pp. 19-27.

Kenny and Syrquin (1999) "Structural Transformations in Tanzania", World Bank Country Study.

Kuznet, S. (1971) "Economic Growth of Nations: Total Output and Production Structure." Cambridge: The Belnap Press of Harvard University Press.

Kuznet, S. (1963) "Quantitative Aspects of the Economic Growth of Nations. Distribution of Income by Size, Economic Development and Cultural Change." Part Two. Vol.11.

Levine, R. and D. Renelt (1992) " A Sensitivity Analysis of Cross - Country Growth Regressions" *American Economic Review*, Vol. 82, 942 - 963.

Lewis, A. (1954) "Economic Development with Unlimited Supplies of Labor." Manchester, Manchester School Press.

Lewis, A. (1958) "Unlimited Supplies of Labor." Further Notes. Manchester, Manchester School.

Lucas, R.E (1988) "On the Mechanics of Economic Development", *Journal of Monetary Economics,* Vol. 22, pp. 3-42.

Malthus, T. (1970) "An Essay on Principles of Population and summary view of the Principles of Population." New York, Penguin Book.

Mankew, N.G., D. Romer and N.D. Weil (1992) "A Contribution to Empirics of Economic Growth." *Quarterly Journal of Economics,* Vol. 107, pp. 407-37.

McRae, H. (1994) "The World in 2020." Boston, Harvard Business School Press.

Meier, G.M. (1964) "Leading Issues in Economics Development." Selected Materials and Commentary, New York, Oxford University Press.

Meier G.M. (1970) "Leading Issues in Economic Development." Second Edition, Oxford, Oxford University Press.

Meier G.M. (1995) "Leading Issues in Economic Development." Sixth Edition, Oxford, Oxford University Press.

Milanzi, M.C. (1995) "The Research Report On Administrative Strategies of Plant Protection in Tanzania." The Case of the Big Four Regions. Institute of Development Management –Mzumbe, Morogoro, Mzumbe Book Project.

Mrema, A. P. (2001) "Investment and Endogenous growth in Tanzania: An-Empirical Investigation." Dar es Salaam, Dar es Salaam University Press.

Nyauhenga, T. W. (2001) "Foreign Aid and Economic Growth in Tanzania: 1970 - 1999, Dar es Salaam, Dar es Salaam University Press.

Parish, A. and D. Bailey (1990) "Techniques of Economic Analysis with Applications." New York, Harvester Wheatsheaf.

Reynolds, L.G. (1985). " Economic Growth in the Third World: 1850 - 1980." New Haven and London, Yale University Press.

Robinson, S. (1971). "The Sources of Growth In Less Developed Countries." A Cross Section Study, *Quarterly Journal of Economics, Vol. 86, pp. 4-13.*

Romer, P.M. (1990)," Endogenous Technological Change". *Journal of Political Economy, Part II*, Vol.98, pp. 571 – 102.

Rostow, W.W. (1960). "The Stages of Economic Growth." Cambridge, Cambridge University Press.

Schultz, T.W. (1961). "Investment in Human Capital." *American Economic Review,* Vol.51, pp. 1 – 17.

Slanlake, G.G. (1979). "Macro-Economics: An Introduction", 2nd Edition, Essex, Longman.

Solow, R.M. (1956) "A Contribution to the Theory of Economic Growth". *Quarterly Journal of Economics,* Vol. 70, pp. 65 – 94.

Solow, R. (1956) "A Contribution to the Theory of Economic Growth." *Quarterly Journal of Economic* Vol.70, pp.65-94.

Streeten. P. (1981) " First Things First." Meeting Basic Needs in Developing Countries, Oxford, Oxford University Press.

Swan, T. (1956) "Economic Growth and Capital Accumulation." *Economic Report,* Vol. 32, pp. 334-61.

Tallman, W. E. and P. Wang (1994) "Human Capital and Endogenous Growth Evidence from Taiwan." *Journal of Monetary Economics,* Vo. 34, pp. 101-24.

Tanzania. (1996) "The Challenge of Reforms: Growth, Incomes and Welfare (In Three Volumes): Vol. 1 Main Report, Country Operations Division. Eastern Africa Department, Africa Region". *World Bank, Repor,.* No. 1482 – TA.

Thirlwall, A.P. (1978) "Growth and Development With Special Reference to Developing Economies". London, Macmillan.

Tinbergen, J. (1952) "On the Theory of Economic Policy." Amsterdam, North - Holland Publishing Company.

Tobin, J. (1972) "The Economy of China: A Tourist view". Nairobi, University of Nairobi.

Todaro, M. (1969) " A Model of Labour Migration and Urban Unemployment In Less Developing Countries." *American Economic Review, Vol.59, pp. 26-37.*

Todaro, M. (1994)."Economic Development In the Third World." London, Longman.

Toussaint, E. and P. Drucker (Eds.) (1995). IMF/World Bank/WTO. "The Free Market Fiasco." Notebooks for Study and Research. Amsterdam/Brussels, International Institute for Research and Education, *No. 24/25.*

UNDP (2001). "Making New Technologies Work for Human Development." *Human Development Report 2001,* New York, Oxford University Press.

Von Freyhold, M. (1979) "Ujamaa Villages in Tanzania: Analysis of Social Experiment". Ibadan/Nairo, Heinemann.

Williams, H.R. and J.D. Huffnagle (Eds.) (1969) "Macro-Economic Theory: Selected Readings" New York, Appleton - Century - Crofts.

World Bank, World Development Report, 1980, Part I and part II.

A World Bank Country Study (2000). "Agriculture in Tanzania Since 1986." Follower or Leader of Growth? Washington DC, World Bank/International Food Policy Research Institute.

A World Bank Country Study (2001). "Tanzania At The Turn Of The Century: From Reforms to Sustained Growth and Poverty Reductions". Washington DC, World Bank.

Zook, D.P. (Ed.) (1962). "Investment in Human Capital in Poor Countries, Foreign Trade and Human Capital". New York, Southern Methodist University.

APPENDICES:

Appendix 1: Results obtained from estimating two separate equations after exhibiting structural break

Dependent Variable: LGDPA
Method: Least Squares
Sample (adjusted): 1979 2000
Included observations: 33 after adjusting endpoints

Variable	Coefficient	Standard Error	t-Statistic	Prob.
C	0.000225	0.011110	0.020257	0.9840
LTIHA	-1.081409	0.230240	-4.696885	0.0001
LTPIA	-0.271592	0.117546	-2.310514	0.0291
LTTA	3.023024	0.117364	25.75761	0.0000
POPA	-0.215661	0.060637	-3.556584	0.0015
INFA	-0.019724	0.003559	-5.541595	0.0000
TDA	0.002872	0.375665	0.007645	0.9940

R-squared	0.999953	Mean dependent var	4.963084
Adjusted R-squared	0.999942	S.D. dependent var	6.667650
Standard Error. of regression	0.050913	Akaike info criterion	-2.931559
Sum squared resid	0.067396	Schwarz criterion	-2.614118
Log likelihood	55.37072	F-statistic	91466.78
Durbin-Watson stat.	2.997920	Prob (F-statistic)	0.000000

Dependent Variable: LGDP
Method: Least Squares
Sample: 1961 2000
Included observations: 40

Variable	Coefficient	Standard Error	t-Statistic	Probability
C	12.24205	0.370107	33.07704	0.0000
LTIH	-0.833885	0.110163	-7.569575	0.0000
LTPI	0.186362	0.111679	1.668738	0.1046
POP	0.440781	0.025526	17.26776	0.0000
INF	-0.063437	0.007359	-8.620784	0.0000
LTT	-7.81E-05	1.58E-05	-4.958375	0.0000
TD	-10.96962	0.346161	-31.68935	0.0000
R-squared	0.999708	Mean dependent var		7.852549
Adjusted R-squared	0.999654	S.D. dependent var		6.602328
Standard error of regression	0.122739	Akaike info criterion		-1.199877
Sum squared resid	0.497144	Schwarz criterion		-0.904323
Log likelihood	30.99754	F-statistic		18802.34
Durbin-Watson stat	1.762664	Prob (F-statistic)		0.000000

128

Dependent Variable: LGDP
Method: Least Squares
Sample (adjusted): 1968 2000
Included observations: 33 after adjusting endpoints

Variable	Coefficient	Standard Error	t-Statistic	Prob.
C	12.94156	0.077588	166.7993	0.0000
LTIH	-0.012425	0.036167	-0.343551	0.7350
LTPI	0.027504	0.022900	1.201062	0.2445
POP	0.037105	0.015023	2.469782	0.0232
INF	0.000381	0.002672	0.142444	0.8882
LTT	-5.02E-06	4.05E-06	-1.239880	0.2301
TD	-0.256781	0.381500	-0.673082	0.5090
LGDPA	-0.823076	0.098360	-8.367995	0.0000
LTIHA	0.265482	0.150393	1.765259	0.0936
LTPIA	0.113866	0.062011	1.836231	0.0820
POPA	-0.000389	0.035451	-0.010983	0.9914
INFA	0.003510	0.002524	1.390722	0.1804
LTTA	-0.365861	0.290090	-1.261199	0.2225
TDA	-0.419726	0.180738	-2.322288	0.0315

R-squared	0.999991	Mean dependent var	9.306120
Adjusted R-squared	0.999985	S.D. dependent var	6.377725
Standard error of regression	0.024414	Akaike info criterion	-4.290913
Sum squared resid	0.011325	Schwarz criterion	-3.656031
Log likelihood	84.80006	F-statistic	167981.1
Durbin-Watson stat	1.599992	Prob (F-statistic)	0.000000

1.2 Results obtained after disaggregating the total trade variable

Dependent Variable: GDP
Included observations: 32 after adjusting endpoints

Variable	Coefficient	Standard Error	t-Statistic	Prob.
C	12.1075.7	57614.73	2.101470	0.0463
LTPI	3.925468	20686.82	1.897570	0.0698
LTIH	1.168950	25966.42	0.450178	0.6566
POP	0.351378	8112.526	2.898454	0.0079
INF	-4.120845	1107.486	-0.066927	0.9472
TD	-7.508290	162447.9	-0.462197	0.6481
LEX	0.256799	0.163382	1.571775	0.1291
LIM	-0.054884	0.073798	-0.743700	0.4643

R-squared	0.988294	Mean dependent var	1111347.
Adjusted R-squared	0.984880	S.D. dependent var	268721.4
S.E. of regression	33042.99	Akaike info criterion	23.86132
Sum squared resid	2.62E+10	Schwarz criterion	24.22776
Log likelihood	-373.7812	F-statistic	289.4647
Durbin-Watson stat	1.084599	Prob (F-statistic)	0.000000

1.2 Plotting the LGDP Residuals

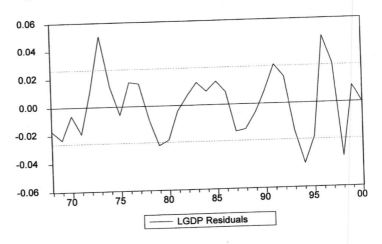

130

2.0 Appendix 2: Examining the behavior of the variables by graphing them

2.1 Plotting the GDP

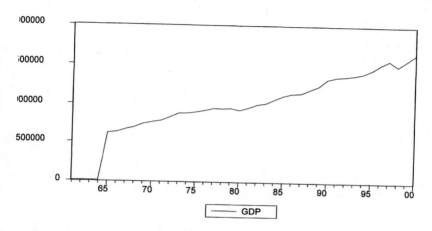

2.2 Plotting the logarithmic values of GDP i.e. LGDP

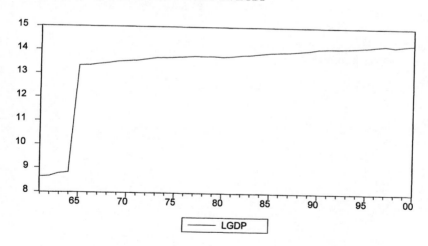

2.3 Plotting the differenced log of GDP i.e. DLGDP

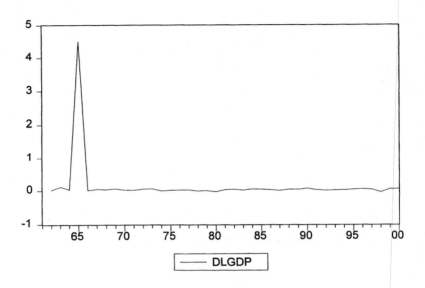

2.4 Plotting the inflation

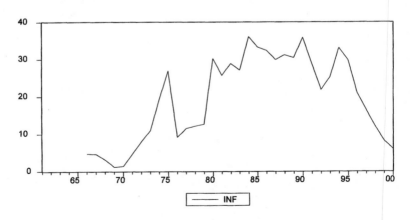

2.5 Differencing the inflation and potting its graph

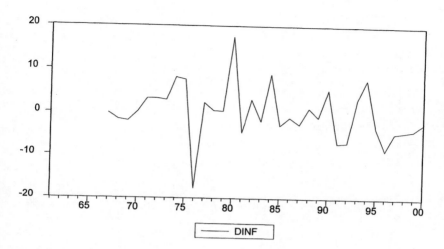

DINF

2.6 Plotting the TPI graph

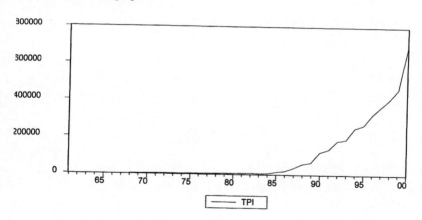

TPI

133

2.7 Plotting the Log of TPI

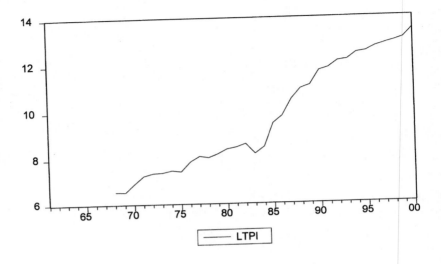

2.8 Plotting the Differenced log of LTPI

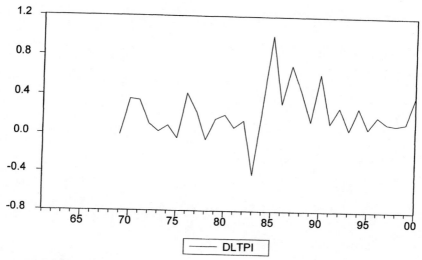

2.9 Plotting the TIH

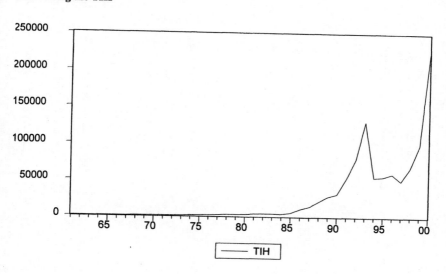

2.10 Plotting the log of TIH

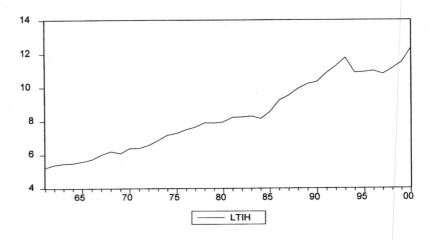

2.11 Plotting the differenced log of TIH

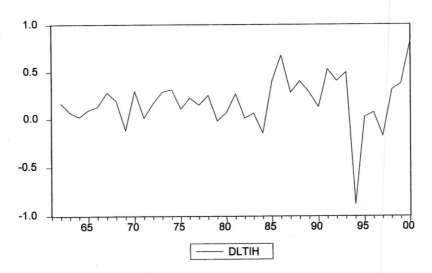

2.12 Plotting the TD variable

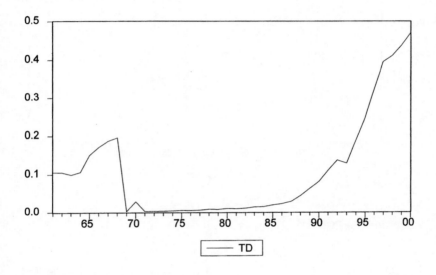

2.13 Plotting the differenced TD variable

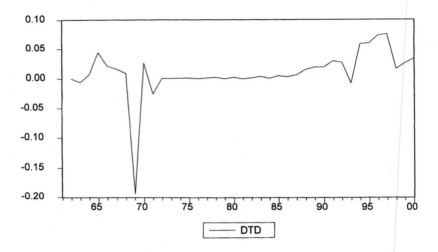

2.14 Plotting the POP variable

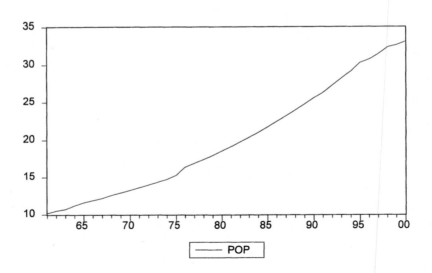

2.15 Plotting the differenced POP

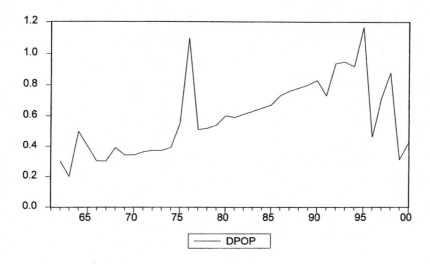

2.16 Plotting the residuals.

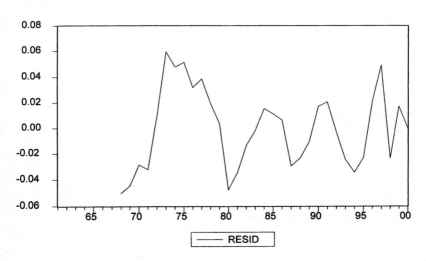

139

Dependent Variable: LGDP
Method: Least Squares
Date: 06/12/02   Time: 16:26
Sample(adjusted): 1968 2000
Included observations: 33 after adjusting endpoints

Variable	Coefficient	Standard Error	t-Statistic	Prob.
LTPI	-0.089000	0.588559	-0.151216	0.8810
LTIH	0.377119	0.637395	0.591657	0.5594
LTT	4.20E-05	0.000118	0.357049	0.7241
POP	-1.098354	0.237970	-4.615508	0.0001
TD	-0.913262	3.898372	-0.234268	0.8167
INF	-0.012388	0.029398	-0.421402	0.6771
LTGE	3.495183	0.440572	7.933279	0.0000
DUM79	-0.662568	0.795534	-0.832859	0.4128

R-squared	-9.476582	Mean dependent var.	13.90557
Adjusted R-squared	-12.410025	S.D. dependent var.	0.250319
Standard error of regression	0.916660	Akaike info criterion	2.871056
Sum squared resid	21.00663	Schwarz criterion	3.233846
Log likelihood	-39.37242	Durbin-Watson stat	1.673861

140

Dependent Variable: LGDP
Method: Least Squares
Date: 06/12/02   Time: 16:29
Sample(adjusted): 1968 1999
Included observations: 32 after adjusting endpoints

Variable	Coefficient	Standard Error	t-Statistic	Prob.
C	12.96000	0.125414	103.3376	0.0000
LTPI	0.034185	0.035074	0.974649	0.0399
LTIH	0.005982	0.030714	0.194760	0.1473
LEX	0.012848	0.037151	0.345843	0.7326
LIMP	-0.022460	0.054071	-0.415371	0.6817
POP	0.031414	0.013665	2.298847	0.0309
TD	-0.244243	0.165968	-1.471622	0.1547
INF	0.000362	0.001165	0.310704	0.7588
LTGE	-4.29E-05	0.036117	-0.001188	0.9991

R-squared	0.983569	Mean dependent var.	13.89265
Adjusted R-squared	0.977854	S.D. dependent var.	0.242891
Standard error of regression	0.036146	Akaike info criterion	-3.570254
Sum squared resid	0.030050	Schwarz criterion	-3.158016
Log likelihood	66.12407	F-statistic	172.1010
Durbin-Watson stat	0.718515	Prob(F-statistic)	0.000000

Wald Test:
Equation: Untitled

Null Hypothesis: C(2)=0

F-statistic	0.949942	Probability	0.339874
Chi-square	0.949942	Probability	0.329734

Null Hypothesis: C(3)=0

F-statistic	0.037932	Probability	0.847291
Chi-square	0.037932	Probability	0.845581

Null Hypothesis: C(4)=0

F-statistic	0.119608	Probability	0.732604
Chi-square	0.119608	Probability	0.729460

Null Hypothesis: C(7)=0

F-statistic	2.165673	Probability	0.154674
Chi-square	2.165673	Probability	0.141123

141

AUTO CORRELATION ANALYSIS

Included observations: 32

Autocorrelation	Partial Correlation		AC	PAC	Q-Statistics	Probability
. |***	. |***	1	0.330	0.330	3.8287	0.050
. |* .	. |* .	2	0.169	0.067	4.8659	0.088
. | .	. | .	3	0.037	-0.042	4.9164	0.178
. |* .	. |* .	4	0.102	0.103	5.3194	0.256
. |** .	. |** .	5	0.240	0.210	7.6488	0.177
. |** .	. |* .	6	0.315	0.195	11.800	0.067
. |***	. |** .	7	0.355	0.214	17.278	0.016
. *| .	***| .	8	-0.085	-0.338	17.605	0.024
. *| .	. *| .	9	-0.141	-0.156	18.549	0.029
. *| .	. *| .	10	-0.135	-0.093	19.446	0.035
. *| .	. **| .	11	-0.156	-0.275	20.699	0.037
. | .	. *| .	12	-0.027	-0.085	20.738	0.054
. | .	. *| .	13	-0.045	-0.058	20.853	0.076
. *| .	. *| .	14	-0.134	-0.081	21.939	0.080
. **| .	. |* .	15	-0.262	0.068	26.339	0.035
. *| .	. |* .	16	-0.169	0.140	28.273	0.029

Chow Breakpoint Test: 1979

F-statistic	3.988125	Probability	0.010449
Log likelihood ratio	40.66643	Probability	0.000006

Recursive Residuals

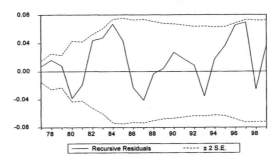

142

Dependent Variable: LGDP
Method: Least Squares
Included observations: 33 after adjusting endpoints

Variable	Coefficient	Standard Error	t-Statistic	P-Value
C	12.89524	0.041585	310.0934	0.0000
LTPI	0.018938	0.016479	1.149208	0.2618
LTIH	0.003992	0.018524	0.215531	0.8312
POP	0.037677	0.006677	5.642638	0.0000
LTT	-4.98E-06	3.46E-06	-1.436217	0.1638
INF	0.002793	0.000982	2.843732	0.0090
TD	-0.332112	0.111862	-2.968956	0.0067
DUM1979	-0.102576	0.025056	-4.093874	0.0004
DUM1997	0.064243	0.029747	2.159646	0.0410

R-squared	0.991800	Mean dependent var.	13.90557
Adjusted R-squared	0.989066	S.D. dependent var.	0.250319
Standard error of regression	0.026175	Akaike info criterion	-4.221058
Sum squared resid	0.016443	Schwarz criterion	-3.812919
Log likelihood	78.64745	F-statistic	362.8376
Durbin-Watson stat	1.437857	Prob (F-statistic)	0.000000

143

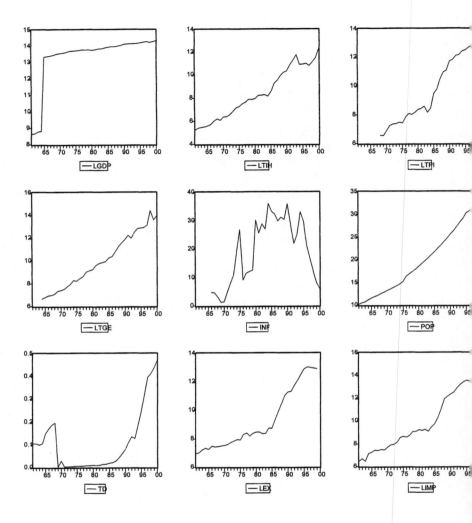

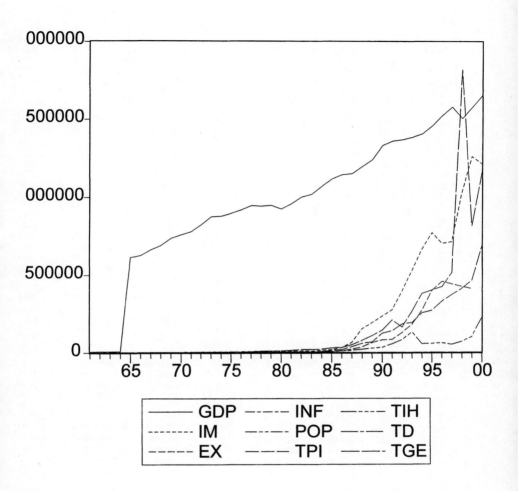

Year	GDP	EX	IM	INF	POP	TGE	TIH	TPI	TD
1961-1	5619	1056.7	650		10.2		187.8		0.105428
1962-1	5773	1119.3	796.3		10.5		222.7		0.105179
1963-1	6514	1371.3	644		10.7		238.8		0.099309
1964-1	6777	1530.9	1262		11.2	777.1	244.3		0.105917
1965-1	615024	1402.5	1410		11.6	884.3	269		0.15
1966-1	626327	1785.2	1694	4.7	11.9	1023.8	306.2		0.171
1967-1	662652	1667.7	1637.6	4.6	12.2	1065	407		0.187
1968-1	690349	1717.7	1833.7	3.1	12.59	1186	492.6	712	0.196
1969-1	736769	1792.4	1710.1	1.2	12.93	1526.7	437.8	704	0.002
1970-1	759289	1852	2274.2	1.4	13.27	1631.4	590.7	1008	0.028
1971-1	778271	1989	2725	4.7	13.63	1780.6	598.5	1425	0.0024
1972-1	824260	2312	2878	8	14	2275.9	708.5	1584	0.0025
1973-1	877065	2581	3479	11	14.37	2785.8	948.5	1624	0.003
1974-1	880589	2861	5258	19.2	14.76	3961.1	1300.8	1776	0.0038
1975-1	899344	2765.3	5694	26.9	15.31	3715.6	1450.9	1693	0.0047
1976-1	921097	4109	5391	9.2	16.41	4702.5	1819.9	2573	0.0046
1977-1	948642	4536.1	6200	11.6	16.92	5563.3	2116	3244	0.0055
1978-1	943862	3671	8798	12.2	17.44	8295	2736.8	3050	0.0078
1979-1	949452	4404	8941	12.7	17.98	9442	2684.6	3566	0.0074
1980-1	927051	4776	10229	30.2	18.58	10230	2876.8	4359	0.0094
1981-1	958242	4806	9739	25.7	19.17	14755	3771.8	4677	0.009
1982-1	1002233	4256	10419	28.9	19.78	17387	3811.9	5401	0.0099
1983-1	1021190	4319	9018	27.1	20.41	18993	4051.4	3534	0.0135
1984-1	1071541	6235	13373	36.1	21.06	20409	3495.3	4713	0.014
1985-1	1119017	6173	16966	33.3	21.73	28509	5252.8	12875	0.0185
1986-1	1147745	11067	29880	32.4	22.46	31710	10313.6	17723	0.0215
1987-1	1154330	19713	61902	29.9	23.22	47871	13702.8	35894	0.0273
1988-1	1201240	33846	150122	31.2	24	75297	20548.9	56578	0.0424
1989-1	1246460	60969	189758	30.4	24.8	106098	27402.6	65021	0.0613
1990-1	1334270	77946	231283	35.9	25.63	140871	31155.2	121098	0.0802
1991-1	1361920	81278	271378	28.8	26.36	207292	52835.3	136572	0.1094
1992-1	1369870	125219	392665	21.9	27.3	161474	79383.4	181113	0.136
1993-1	1386400	178274	531742	25.2	28.25	263413	130392.2	189858	0.1281
1994-1	1408120	265912	666258	33.1	29.17	374962	54161.75	251834	0.1866
1995-1	1458400	395390.1	770779	29.8	30.34	398024	55370.64	268156	0.2462
1996-1	1524670	455419.1	702441	21	30.8	420522	59575.9	326032	0.3198
1997-1	1578300	438180	713592	16.4	31.51	515390	49772.55	368783	0.395
1998-1	1505830	421449.8	1036440	12.1	32.39	1820338	68274.12	409908	0.4111
1999-1	1577291	407118.1	1265767	8.2	32.7	816706	99600.7	464739	0.437
2000-1	1654410	531633. 3	1217533	6	33.12	1168779	223792.4	689619	0.47

Transforming the variables into logarithms in attempt to stabilize them.

	LGDP	LEX	LIMP	LTIH	LTPI	DINF	DPOP
1961-1	8.633909	6.962906	6.476972	5.235378			
1962-1	8.660947	7.020459	6.679976	5.405826			0.3
1963-1	8.781709	7.223514	6.467699	5.475626			0.2
1964-1	8.82129	7.333611	7.140453	5.498397			0.5
1965-1	13.32942	7.246012	7.251345	5.594711			0.4
1966-1	13.34763	7.487286	7.434848	5.724238			0.3
1967-1	13.40401	7.419201	7.400987	6.008813		-0.1	0.3
1968-1	13.44495	7.448741	7.514091	6.199697	6.568078	-1.5	0.39
1969-1	13.51003	7.491311	7.444307	6.081762	6.556778	-1.9	0.34
1970-1	13.54014	7.524021	7.729384	6.381308	6.915723	0.2	0.34
1971-1	13.56483	7.595387	7.910224	6.394427	7.261927	3.3	0.36
1972-1	13.62224	7.745868	7.964851	6.56315	7.367709	3.3	0.37
1973-1	13.68434	7.855932	8.1545	6.854882	7.392648	3	0.37
1974-1	13.68835	7.958926	8.567506	7.170735	7.482119	8.2	0.39
1975-1	13.70942	7.924904	8.647168	7.279939	7.434257	7.7	0.55
1976-1	13.73332	8.320935	8.592486	7.506537	7.852828	-17.7	1.1
1977-1	13.76279	8.419823	8.732305	7.657283	8.084562	2.4	0.51
1978-1	13.75774	8.208219	9.08228	7.914545	8.022897	0.6	0.52
1979-1	13.76364	8.390268	9.098403	7.895287	8.1792	0.5	0.54
1980-1	13.73976	8.471359	9.232982	7.964434	8.379998	17.5	0.6
1981-1	13.77286	8.47762	9.183894	8.235308	8.450412	-4.5	0.59
1982-1	13.81774	8.356085	9.251386	8.245883	8.594339	3.2	0.61
1983-1	13.83648	8.370779	9.106978	8.306818	8.170186	-1.8	0.63
1984-1	13.88461	8.737934	9.500993	8.159174	8.45808	9	0.65
1985-1	13.92796	8.72794	9.738967	8.566517	9.463043	-2.8	0.67
1986-1	13.95331	9.311723	10.30494	9.241219	9.782619	-0.9	0.73
1987-1	13.95903	9.889034	11.03331	9.525355	10.48833	-2.5	0.76
1988-1	13.99886	10.42958	11.9192	9.930563	10.94338	1.3	0.78
1989-1	14.03582	11.01812	12.1535	10.21839	11.08247	-0.8	0.8
1990-1	14.10389	11.26377	12.3514	10.34674	11.70436	5.5	0.83
1991-1	14.12441	11.30563	12.51127	10.87493	11.82461	-7.1	0.73
1992-1	14.13023	11.73782	12.88071	11.28204	12.10688	-6.9	0.94
1993-1	14.14222	12.09108	13.18391	11.7783	12.15403	3.3	0.95
1994-1	14.15777	12.49092	13.40943	10.89973	12.43653	7.9	0.92
1995-1	14.19285	12.88763	13.55516	10.9218	12.49932	-3.3	1.17
1996-1	14.23729	13.02897	13.46232	10.99501	12.69475	-8.8	0.46
1997-1	14.27186	12.99039	13.47807	10.81522	12.81796	-4.6	0.71
1998-1	14.22485	12.95146	13.8513	11.13129	12.92369	-4.3	0.88
1999-1	14.27122	12.91686	14.05119	11.50892	13.04923	-3.9	0.31
2000-1	14.31896		14.01234	12.31847	13.44389	-2.2	0.42

147

Key to Abbreviations:

GDP- Gross Domestic Product in 1992 prices

TPI = Infrastructural & non-infrastructural public investments defined as capital formation in land improvement, roads, water, energy and transport as well as communication services and Capital formation in rural own housing respectively.

EX = Volume of Exports trade in Tanzanian currency

IM   = Volume of Import trade in Tanzanian currency

INF = Inflation growth rate.

POP = Population Growth rate

TGE = Total Government Expenditures (Nominal)

TIH = Investment in Human capital proxied as government expenditures in education and health sector.

TD   = Tax Distortion proxied as a ratio of Revenue collection to GDP

Source: Various Government publications, International Financial Statistics and Various CD ROMs